Bad Meetings Happen to Good People

How to Run Meetings That Are Effective, Focused, and Produce Results

Leigh Espy

Blue Room Press
Memphis, Tennessee

For more information, go to: LeighEspy.com
Published by Blue Room Press
ISBN: 978-0-9993262-0-6

CONTENTS

ACKNOWLEDGEMENTS

When I set out to write on the topic of meetings, it didn't start as a book. It started as several blog posts and templates that grew into something larger. Once I committed to writing a book, I didn't realize just how much work would be required. It was the support and assistance of friends and family that helped turn this idea to write a book into a reality.

I want to thank Annette Mertens, Chris Lambert, Jennifer Balink, and Katie Shepherd for their input and suggestions.

Also, a huge thank you to all who contributed stories. Those experiences will hopefully make the book richer to the reader.

I'm grateful to those who engaged in many hours of conversation about this topic and shared personal experiences and support.

A huge thank you to my editors Kirsten Johnson and Jessica Huntley. Kirsten provided massive support also by guiding me through this process. I didn't know that there was so much I didn't know about writing and publishing a book. I likely wouldn't have made it to the finish line if Kirsten didn't help get me there.

And to my amazing family, Stephen and Sophia, who supported me through this process in so many ways. I'm a lucky girl to have them.

INTRODUCTION

Every week, many hours are wasted in poorly run meetings. My goal in this book is to compile to-the-point tactics to give you the tools to run great meetings that are focused and effective.

If you follow the steps outlined in this book, you'll not only run meetings that produce results, but you'll move through them with ease and confidence. Your co-workers will marvel at your leadership and ability to navigate common meeting challenges. Over time you'll develop a reputation for holding meetings that are productive and valuable.

Don't underestimate the value of running great meetings. Not only will everyone appreciate your skill, but it can boost your career. Let the guidance in this book take the stress out of meetings, increase your value to your organization, and help your leadership skills shine through.

"Luck is a matter of preparation meeting opportunity."
Lucius Annaeus Seneca

TRIAL BY FIRE

It was Tuesday, and my stomach hurt. Just like every Tuesday.

That's because on Tuesday mornings my team had our Genesis project meeting. Inevitably, something would go wrong.

It might be that we didn't have the key decision-makers present, or the discussion veered off topic, and we ran out of time, not getting to all the agenda items. Or, nothing had moved forward since our last meeting.

I felt like we'd spent an hour talking, yet accomplishing nothing.

I came to dread these meetings.

Not always, of course. Sometimes they went well, and I walked away feeling good about the meeting and the project.

We had enough bad meetings to generate a feeling of dread about them.

I was the meeting facilitator, for goodness sake. It was my fault, as the leader, that these meetings didn't meet my expectations and hopes. I could only imagine what the participants must have felt about these meetings.

I knew they were judging me and my ability to lead this meeting to be productive. They must have dreaded these meetings even more than I did, and I'd heard what people said about other meetings.

"Ugh! Not another meeting."

"What a waste of time. When can we get to our desks to get some real work done?"

"Didn't we have that same conversation in the last meeting? Why are we spending time going through this again?"

"Do you realize how much company money we just wasted in that room?"

Something had to change. If the meeting was bad for me, it was bad for the team and the project. None of us wanted to go on like this.

I looked at the various components of the meeting and identified ways to improve. Over time the meetings ran more smoothly and became more productive—We had real results out of each meeting. Not only did my stomach aches subside, but I came to look forward to Tuesday mornings. It became a personal challenge to see just how successful I could make each meeting.

I began to get compliments on how effective my meetings were. People noticed.

Over the years, I've continued to use the approach I took with the Genesis project meetings and apply it to all my meetings. It's served me well.

I realized at some point that surely I'm not the only one who has ever felt that way. When polling friends and co-workers, I hear the same dreaded comments about poorly run meetings. I've attended poorly-run meetings and thought some of these things myself, especially now that I know how valuable a well-run meeting can be.

I decided to compile what I've learned over the years into this book in the hopes it will keep someone from going through the same stress I did.

A poorly run meeting is a waste of time. There's the opportunity cost. Instead of sitting in a poorly run meeting, you could have been in a conversation generating reliable solutions, identifying next steps to move a project forward, or any number of valuable activities.

The information in this book provides the tools needed to lead productive and valuable meetings. Use it as your guide for what to do each step of the way to lead meetings that get results. You'll be able to lead the group through targeted meeting goals and come away with real value. You'll know how to navigate tricky situations that may have derailed you in the past. Plus, you'll do it calmly and confidently while growing in your career.

You'll come to be known as someone who can lead and get results. Use these opportunities to grow in your career. Leading meetings is an excellent way to get noticed and begin to take on larger projects if desired.

Everything won't go perfectly every time, but if you have a reputation as one who treats meetings as seriously as others hope you do, they'll see you as a competent leader they can trust.

A poorly run meeting not only wastes time, but has an opportunity cost as well.

My Background

As a project manager with many years of experience, I've run hundreds of meetings. I've worked in a variety of settings with different teams and various dynamics. I've worked with teams who had great rapport, and with teams who came to the table grudgingly. I've experienced the problems mentioned in this book, so I know firsthand how it can feel to find yourself in these uncomfortable situations.

I've coached at-risk youth and their families in emotionally charged, tense situations. While working for a home-based program targeting delinquent, unruly, and neglected children at risk of out-of-home placement, I learned the high value of soft-skills and communication.

I've learned the value of embracing challenges as opportunities to grow and improve. I shifted my perspective on tough meetings. Instead of viewing them as stressful events, I have come to see them as opportunities to improve. I embraced the challenge to hold the best meetings I could. I wanted people to walk away with the feeling that we'd accomplished something, and ready to take the next steps to move our project forward.

I'm not perfect, and I still encounter problems in my meetings. There are still challenges, but I'm prepared for them now. I want you to be, too. Because time is precious, and your project is important, your next meeting is an opportunity for you to shine.

HOW TO USE THIS BOOK

The book is organized into two parts. The first part covers specific activities to do before, during, and after your meeting for the best results. The second part covers other valuable considerations that contribute to productive meetings, such as how to handle common meeting challenges that can derail your best intentions. Select a section and choose a few actions to take to improve your meeting skills. Then continue to adopt new practices to continually improve your meetings.

All the steps and suggestions in this book won't apply to every meeting you hold. Use your best judgment for what actions will produce the highest return. For example, if you're holding a short project discussion with two co-workers, you'll want to have a clear idea of the meeting intent and focus, and come away with agreement on post–meeting action items. You likely won't need to time-box the agenda or worry much about room layout.

Honestly, there's nothing revolutionary or new here. Yet, for some reason, bad meetings continue to happen even for those with the best intentions.

Apply the tactics in this book yourself, and share it with your teammates. By continually improving your meetings, you'll save time, money, and increase the value of the time spent in meetings.

WHO CAN BENEFIT FROM READING THIS BOOK?

Can You Relate?

Mike's boss has asked him to schedule a meeting to discuss the next steps in a project they're considering. Mike agrees to do it, even as he's filled with a sense of dread.

Mike knows he needs to start running meetings to broaden his visibility. He wants to grow in his career and needs to increase his experience, especially if he's to be trusted to run teams and move projects forward.

The idea of running a meeting puts Mike's stomach in knots. He doesn't want to embarrass himself in front of his teammates or his boss.

He's heard his co-workers complain of useless, time-wasting meetings, and he doesn't want to be blamed for another one of those.

His anxiety grows.

Sarah, on the other hand, has run meetings before, but she still dreads getting in front of the group. She has been in too many meetings that seem to go nowhere and are a waste of time. She's had her meetings derailed, accomplishing nothing. Sarah knows meetings can be a useful tool, but wonders why her meetings sometimes go nowhere.

If you are in either of these situations, this book is for you. Leading meetings is an excellent way to get more visibility and leadership opportunity. It provides a chance to show your ability to direct a group to reach specific outcomes. When you drive a project forward efficiently with a great meeting, you show peers and bosses they can trust you to lead.

Conversely, running a meeting poorly can be disastrous. It can expose your lack of understanding and inability to handle the responsibility that has been entrusted to you.

Tim Robertson shared a story demonstrating how running meetings badly can have severe consequences.

We had a large software development team that was split across the US and Argentina. We had technical leads, engineers, designers, and product managers on the team. Managing the work was time intensive.

The product was complex, and the project was moving quickly, so it was hard to maintain coordination of all the work.

We hired a project manager. All he did was set up meetings. Each day the meetings would grow. He'd add more and more people. And I'd frequently find myself in hour-long meetings that had NOTHING to do with me or my work.

Most of the time, I'd tune out and just work, along with the handful of other people there who didn't need to be involved.

He was fond of saying, "Let's get everybody in a room." This can be a reasonable strategy when used wisely. But when you just invite everyone to every meeting and don't help drive any resolution in those meetings, you're wasting everyone's time.

His meetings were scoped to try to resolve a specific issue and started with a reasonable premise. But during the meeting, they went all over the place. He never seemed to gain enough understanding to be able to control or manage the meeting. And these meetings continued to be an unproductive waste of the team's valuable time.

It was so bad that we fired him.

If you want to run meetings well to move your projects forward, demonstrate your leadership skills, and make your bosses and team love you, then the guidance in this book will help.

We'll cover, step-by-step, what to do from the moment you decide to meet, all the way to the days following the meeting, to make sure you and your attendees get the most from each meeting.

Never underestimate the value of running great meetings. Everyone will appreciate your skill, and it can boost your career.

Do I Really Need to Hold a Meeting?

When teams want to share information, often the default action is to schedule a meeting.

Are meetings always necessary?

There are other ways to communicate. Depending on the situation and culture of your organization, some executives insist on status being shared in a meeting format.

If you're sending information one-way only, you might find that the best way to share your latest project status or updates could by email or via team collaboration tools.

Determining your intent is an important first step in deciding if you need to have a   meeting. Good reasons to have a meeting include solving a problem, making a decision, solidifying a plan, gathering ideas, or sharing information. Let's look at each.

Solving a problem may require bringing a group of people together. It could be a business problem or a project risk. You may need to address a performance issue in the organization and bring together representatives to apply their expertise to create a solution. The problem may be small enough to solve with only one meeting, or it may need a series of sessions for full resolution.

If there is a **decision to be made**, you may need to bring a team together for discussion to resolve the issue. In this type of meeting, ensure that you have those with the right level of authority in attendance.

Planning meetings are usually collaborative and involve a group working together to develop a plan. To determine a different way of doing something or generate ideas, a brainstorming meeting can be valuable.

Information sharing meetings can provide a number of different information flows. There may be times when you need to gather information from a group of people, such as a focus group or representatives from different areas to give input that will guide decision-making. As the facilitator, it is your job to keep control of the group to ensure it stays productive.

Status meetings are specific forms of information sharing meetings. These allow stakeholders to gather information and give them the opportunity to answer questions. Some stakeholders and managers may want updates via email only, and others specifically want the opportunity to discuss progress and ask questions in a meeting setting. The key to making these meetings valuable is to provide targeted information and ensuring that the group stays on track.

There are times when email is sufficient for sharing information. At other times, you may need to share sensitive information or information that will likely generate many questions. In these situations, it can be helpful to provide that information face-to-face.

For example, I worked on a team that faced the risk of layoffs. The Director brought us together periodically to share updates and answer questions. It was an informal meeting, and he did his best to put everyone at ease and open the floor for questions. This was a much better forum than simply sending an email with his latest update. It showed respect for the team and an effort to handle a delicate matter with the attention and gravity it deserved.

When considering whether to hold a meeting, make sure you understand the reason why you're bringing a group together.

Next time you consider holding a meeting, ask yourself if the purpose justifies bringing a group of people together. If so, then do it. If not, challenge the common assumption that a meeting is always your best path to meet your goal.

And, when you do schedule a meeting, make it count.

PART 1:

THE BASICS—

BEFORE, DURING, AND AFTER

A GUIDE FOR EACH STEP OF YOUR MEETING

Holding a successful meeting includes more than sending invitations and showing up. To get the most value from your meeting, there are actions to take each step of the way. This section explains the activities needed to ensure you hold a meeting that produces results.

This may seem like a lot of work, but the amount of effort needed will be determined by the importance and complexity of the task at hand. If you're bringing together a team to plan an urgent project with a tight timeline, or gathering a group of executives to deliver status on a critical initiative, you'll likely need more preparation than if the meeting is a weekly check-in with peers.

Use this section as a guide. If you're not doing all the activities listed, and your meetings aren't going well, decide which actions from the list will improve the quality of your session. At least a few of these actions should always be done. Other times, it may be beneficial to use all the listed ideas. You should always identify your goal for holding a meeting. Other activities might only be needed for particular situations. Assess for your particular circumstances, but do what is necessary to make your meeting focused and productive.

"By failing to prepare, you are preparing to fail."
Benjamin Franklin

BEFORE

Planning Your Meeting

There can be quite a bit of advance work that goes into a meeting that will depend on the audience and the meeting goals.

There will be times when the group is already well prepared to discuss a topic, so few advance actions are needed.

Conversely, there are situations when you're bringing together a group who may not have background information on what you'll be discussing, who may be new to the team or need more information on a decision that is expected.

It can take a good deal of work to make sure everyone comes to the table ready to address the meeting goal. If you put in the time upfront, your meeting is far more likely to be productive and valuable.

When you have prepared well for your meeting, you'll be able to lead it more calmly. You'll be more confident, and your peers will see you as more competent. You'll earn trust and achieve greater leadership opportunities if desired.

Imagine these two scenarios:

First Scenario:

You arrive at the meeting room and sit down with your printed agendas. You're feeling flustered because the meeting is scheduled to start in five minutes and the copy machine jammed just as you were making copies. You were finally able to print them and get to the meeting room before your attendees arrived. You reach over to the conference phone to dial in and find that you've forgotten the conference access codes. Then you realize that you need to set up the projector, but due to the printer delay, you don't have enough time to get everything done before your designated start time.

You look up the meeting conference information and work frantically to get it all set up as the participants go in search of chairs because your room doesn't have enough to accommodate everyone.

Finally, they all take a seat and make small talk, while the clock ticks well past the start time. You finally get the projector and conference call set up, but by now you're embarrassed and distressed, and it shows in your frantic behavior. The meeting is off to a poor start, which affects your performance for the rest of the meeting.

And, yes, others notice.

You didn't send an agenda or supporting documentation to the attendees in advance, so they are unprepared for the discussion. They ask for more background information on the topics you thought they knew about already. You end up having the same conversation you had in the last meeting. The meeting ends with everyone feeling like they've had a pleasant conversation, but nothing was accomplished.

Alternate Scenario:

You arrive at the meeting room 15 minutes early and place printouts on the table. You're not bothered by printer problems since you made copies early in the day and had plenty of time to handle it. You visited the room in advance, and know that it has everything you need.

Calmly, you dial into the conference call and set up the projector in the peace of an empty room.

When the participants arrive, you welcome them warmly.

At the designated start time, you bring the group's attention to the meeting purpose and begin the meeting. You're calm and focused, and the group has confidence in your leadership skills.

As you start, you remind the group of the meeting purpose. You sent supporting information in advance and had several conversations to prepare attendees for the work in this meeting. As you move you through the agenda, the group makes decisions and agrees to the next steps. When you leave, the group has achieved the meeting goal, and attendees compliment you on a productive meeting.

Can you see the difference in these two scenarios?

The work you do in advance of the meeting can positively affect the meeting itself. Make the investment, and it will pay off.

"Success depends upon previous preparation, and without such preparation, there is sure to be failure."
Confucius

Meeting Purpose

When planning your meeting, ask yourself why you're bringing the group together.

- Is it simply because your team meets every two weeks?

- Are you brainstorming to generate ideas?

- Do you need a decision?

- Are you working on something with a tangible outcome, such as a document or new process?

Before sending meeting invitations, have a clear understanding of what you hope to accomplish. If you need to gain consensus, solve a problem, or make team decisions, understanding this in advance will help you create a targeted agenda and invite the right participants.

Be clear about how you want to use the meeting time and the value you hope to achieve from it. It's not desirable to bring together a room full of people simply because it's time to have a meeting. If there's no clear agenda or goal, it will be a poor use of everyone's time. Be clear on the meeting goal.

If the intent of your meeting is to share information, ask yourself if it can be shared via a different channel instead. Email or other types of communication work without taking as much time. Getting multiple people together in a room translates to real costs. Use those resources wisely.

Think about your meeting and how it will benefit the project or topic for which it was scheduled. How can you best use this time to move your project or team forward?

If it's a regularly scheduled status meeting, consider how to get the most value from the time. Is it the appropriate length? Is the meeting frequency correct? Are the right people included?

To make sure you know why you're having the meeting, ask yourself the following questions:

What items do we need to address in the meeting?

• What results do we want to accomplish?

Consider what results or answers you want from the group by the end of the meeting. Be very clear on the desired outcome.

Ask Yourself: By the end of the meeting, the group will have _____.

When you can answer this question, you'll know you've identified your purpose and focus.

If you've been asked by your boss or someone else to schedule the meeting, and you're not clear on the goal, ask. Having that conversation will ensure you are all in alignment on the meeting goals.

Meeting Length

Parkinson's Law states "work expands so as to fill the time available for its completion." If you schedule a one-hour meeting for something you could accomplish in 30 minutes, you'll likely fill the entire hour.

There is no hard rule that all meetings must last one hour. If you need to bring a group together to make a quick decision, schedule the meeting duration accordingly. Make sure everyone is well prepared to accomplish the task in the scheduled time by providing necessary supporting materials. This is covered more in a later section.

Ask Yourself: What is the shortest amount of time I can allocate to meet the goal(s) of my meeting?

The Agenda

The agenda is a critical component of your meeting. It provides focus and organization. It tells others what to expect, and it will help you keep the group focused if people stray off topic.

To create your agenda, start with the meeting intent. The agenda items should be relevant to the meeting's purpose. Consider what is needed to cover to accomplish the meeting's goal.

State the meeting purpose clearly at the top of the page, above the bulleted agenda list. It should be a brief statement of the purpose or intended outcome. This allows everyone to arrive prepared and helps keep the discussion on-track. It should be a statement that clearly identifies what intended value you hope to gain from the meeting.

List agenda items, individually, as a brief bullet point. Aim for less than a full line. State these as outcomes whenever possible, rather than simply the topic. Begin each line with an action verb, leading to the desired result, such as "decide" or "resolve." Examples: "address outstanding vendor billing" or "determine event location."

If attendees are focused on goals, rather than discussion, they will come prepared to pay attention and provide their input. It forces you, as the meeting facilitator, to identify the goal of each agenda item and lead the discussion accordingly.

Don't include details about each item on the agenda. If you need to provide supplemental information, include it separately.

Place higher priority items at the beginning of the meeting, first on the agenda. Save less essential items for the end. That way, if you run out of time, you'll have covered the most important things.

A few potential exceptions to this recommendation:

If an attendee can't stay for the entire session and is presenting information to the group, put her first on the agenda. For example, if the accounting representative needs to share the latest budget numbers, but can only stay for 15 minutes, allow her to present first.

If your group historically churns for extended periods of time on an issue, and you have a simple, straightforward item that will take less than five minutes to address, try putting it first so you can get momentum by resolving something quickly. For example, share a quick update from the last Director communication (short agenda item #1) before addressing a larger meeting topic (longer agenda item #2).

If others will present or lead part of the discussion, make sure they know they are on the agenda. Never blindside anyone by adding them to the agenda without their knowledge. Be clear of their topic and time needs. If multiple people will lead different agenda items, put their name by each item as appropriate.

Don't put too many topics into an agenda. Be realistic with your expectations for the time allotted. If you find that you have too many items on your agenda, you have more than one meeting. In these situations, consider the following approaches:

Determine logical ways to group the agenda items into separate meetings. You could have one meeting on one week and a separate meeting the following week. This might allow you to invite participants more targeted to the topics you're focused on specifically.

Form subcommittees to address separate items and have them report back.

Delegate someone to take one of the agenda items and handle it outside of the meeting. The responsible delegate can then address the item and report the results to the team at the next meeting.

Items that can be handled by email communication (sharing progress status on a side item) can be done separately.

Don't load the agenda with lots of text – keep it clear and easy to read, at-a-glance with lots of white space.

List the time allotted for each item so that you can stay on target. This helps attendees know how much time will be given to each agenda item. If you have 10 minutes next to one item, and 30 minutes next to another, it helps set attendee expectations for how the meeting will flow.

Communicate beforehand with each person presenting to make sure they know, not only that they are responsible for an agenda item, but how much time is allotted and if they have any special needs, such as a projector, white board, or other equipment.

Meeting Agenda – STAR Project

Date/Time: Wednesday, 11/08/17, 9:00am – 10:00am CST

Location: Room 246 / Web Conference Meeting ID 25438

Invited: Grace Woods, Nancy Young, Sanjay Dutt, Bruce Richmond, Mike Tanner, Ed Martinez, Angela Diaz

---

Meeting Purpose: Finalize Focus Group Details

AGENDA

- Decide which Teams to include in Focus Groups

- Finalize Team Schedules

Ask Yourself:

Is the meeting purpose stated clearly at the top of the agenda?

Is the agenda clear and representative of what we'll cover?

Am I allowing the right amount of time for each agenda item?

Have I communicated clearly with people who will be responsible for agenda items?

The Participants

Now that you know the specific goal of the meeting identify who to have in attendance to achieve that goal. Remember, the participants needed will vary depending on your desired outcome.

If the intent is to produce a decision, make sure you have the decision-makers there. A junior staff member can't provide a decision if it needs to be made by a Director-level staff person. In that case, make sure you invite the decision-making Director.

If the intent is to get feedback on a solution, have adequate representation from the various desired target areas. Include customer representatives who will use the solution day-to-day.

If you need input from stakeholders for guiding the direction of your plan, invite those stakeholders.

Ask yourself who really needs to be there.

Don't invite people who won't have any contribution or be affected by the topics discussed. It's not a good use of their time, and they'll wonder why they've been invited.

If you're not sure, who needs to participate, get input from your boss or someone else in the organization who can guide you.

One thing to keep in mind: if you are bringing together a group of individual contributors for honest, open input, don't invite upper management. Bringing higher-level executives or management into the room will cause the other participants to edit their contributions. They are less likely to speak as openly. Create a safe space for them to speak freely. This means providing them anonymity regarding their comments, and respect for the opinions they share.

Ask Yourself: Have I invited the appropriate people to my meeting?

The Right Number of Participants

It can be helpful to limit the number of attendees if you need to get a decision.

This guidance may sound contradictory to the previous point of getting stakeholder representation. However, if you have too many people in your meeting, it often won't be productive and can lose focus. It can slow you down, especially if the attendees are new to the topic.

If you have a status meeting or you're providing a solution demo, the number of participants isn't as much of a concern. Conversely, if the group needs to make a decision, too many participants can bog down discussion and make it difficult to gain consensus or reach a resolution. You may find at the end of your meeting that you've not accomplished your meeting goals.

In a nutshell, get the right decision-makers and don't fill the room with those whose vote won't count.

Ask Yourself: Who needs to attend the meeting for it to be successful?

Meeting Space

Make sure the meeting space you've selected supports your requirements. You don't want to start your meeting unprepared and flustered if the room can't accommodate your needs.

Consider this scenario: You arrive at the meeting and find that there's not enough seating, so you borrow chairs from nearby rooms and shove them up against the walls. As you pull your projector out of the case, you see that the nearest power outlet is across the room, not nearly close enough to be able to plug in. You made some copies of your presentation, but you're flustered by now and running behind due to scavenging for chairs. As you dial in on the conference phone, you realize that the call-in attendees won't be able to hear anyone speaking who is sitting against the wall. You're not off to a good start and stressed out already.

To avoid problems, such as these, run through all your meeting room needs beforehand. It's easy to miss things, so go through this list below and make sure you've considered everything.

Checklist for Possible Meeting Room Needs:

- **Remote attendees** make sure the room has the audio components that will allow remote participants to both hear the discussion clearly and be heard by others. Well-placed conference phones will be necessary for everyone to participate fully.

- **Dry-erase board:** If you need whiteboard space for creating diagrams or lists (or any other purpose) ensure you'll have enough. Take your own markers and erasers! There may not be any in the room, and if there are, they probably don't work well.

- **Seating:** Make sure the room can accommodate the number invited. The seating layout should support your meeting intent. For example, if you want to encourage discussion, have attendees seated facing each other rather than in straight classroom-like rows. If you are providing a demo or presentation to a large group, then chairs set in rows would work well.

- **Projector:** If you need to use a projector, check the room to make necessary accommodations. If there's no built-in audio/visual equipment, bring a projector with you. Make sure there's a place for the projector and equipment, along with a suitable projection area. Make sure the projector cord can reach the electrical outlet. You may need to bring an extension cord.

- **Space:** If you have a large group that needs to move around during activities, make sure there's room to get around. For example, if you'll be splitting up into breakout groups for small group discussion, you'll need space for this.

- **Electrical outlets:** If your group will be meeting for several hours and using laptops, they'll need access to electrical outlets. It's helpful to know that your meeting room has them. If you're bringing a projector, you'll need a place to plug it in. I've walked into rooms in which the only electrical outlets were several feet away from the conference table. I luckily had plenty of time to run back to my office, down the hall, to grab an extension cord.

- **Charging stations:** If you're hosting a long meeting, such as an all-day work-session, a few extra charging stations could be helpful.

- **Food or beverages:** If you'll be providing breakfast or lunch during the meeting, make sure there's room for it, along with a table on which to place it. You'll need a garbage can or two for any disposable plates, cups, napkins, and other refuse. Let the attendees know in the invitation that you'll provide food or beverages. You could list it in the agenda. For example, if your meeting is a longer working session: Coffee & pastries 8:30 – 9:00 am.

I've made it a practice to bring a projector along even if the room has one built-in. (An extension cord won't hurt either.) There have been times when I couldn't get the on-site installed projector to work, and couldn't reach technical staff for support. It only took this happening once for me to start the practice of having a backup projector. I've needed it more than once, and have never regretted having it.

Ask Yourself: Did I review my pre-meeting list and have I addressed all the meeting needs?

Preparing For Your Meeting

You've determined the meeting goals, identified the right participants, found the right location, and created your agenda. Yet, there are still several items to do before the day of your meeting to ensure the best results.

Don't worry. The investment will pay off when your meeting day arrives. Both you and your co-workers will be much better prepared, and they'll appreciate you for it.

Meeting Invitations

Allow plenty of notice for attendees when you send the invitation. This isn't always possible, but when you can it will be easier for all involved. If your audience is made up of directors or higher-level executives, you'll likely need even more lead time to get on their calendars. For Directors and above, you may need to work through administrative assistants to coordinate meeting dates and times to get on their calendars. This formality depends on the protocol of your organization.

When sending the invitation, check the invitees' availability to ensure maximum participation (if possible, do this through your scheduling software).

Make sure that attendees know the meeting location and include instructions on how participants can access the session remotely if needed. Add links to webinars and conference access numbers so that they are easy to find and use.

If your meeting is being held off-site at an unfamiliar location, include the physical address in the invitation, with any necessary access instructions or directions to the site. For example, if the building has an access code needed for entry or special parking instructions, include those in the body of the meeting invitation. Post signs guiding people from the parking lot and main entrance to the meeting room. Your attendees will appreciate your help and consideration.

Ask Yourself: Am I allowing enough lead time for invitees to prepare and attend?

Have I provided conference access information for remote attendees?

Meeting Documents

- **Meeting Agenda:** Distribute the meeting agenda as early as you can. If participants need to prepare for any items, they need enough lead-time to do so. Adjust the advance lead time to accommodate the agenda items and schedules of the participants. That way, members will come to the table ready to address the topics listed.

- **Background Information:** If people need background information or other documentation to review before the meeting, provide it to them in advance. Give them at least two days to review it. If possible, and your meeting software and company policies allow, attach it to your meeting request.

There are situations where it is advisable to send documents and other backing materials separately from the emailed meeting invitation.

Anne Marie: My boss (and others) had asked me to send those materials separately so they can delete the email once they have downloaded the information. They told me it took too much space in his email.

- **Presentations:** If your meeting requires a presentation, such as a PowerPoint deck, allow yourself enough time to create it. If you need someone else to review and provide feedback, build in adequate time for the reviewer and time for yourself to make necessary changes.

Don't wait until the last minute to throw something together. It will result in poor quality and add stress to your day.

Attendees

Ask invitees to confirm their attendance to gauge the number of participants. If only three of your 15 invitees can participate, you need to adjust your plans. If you find out that a conflict has come up for many, there's no reason to bring together only a few and then reschedule the same meeting for the following week.

If you've scheduled your meeting during a time many people take vacations, be aware that it's going to make your job that much harder. Holidays, end of the fiscal year, and school breaks are prime times for people to be unavailable. At these times, it's even more important to confirm who can and cannot attend. If people haven't responded to your invitation, nor do they have an "out of office" message, send out an email asking for responses. If most invitees can't be there, consider alternatives.

If the meeting is simply a status report, sending out a presentation or report providing the information you need to communicate might be sufficient, instead of having the meeting.

If you need to have face-time with the invitees, move the meeting date to accommodate their schedules. If you don't, you'll wind up simply having to repeat the meeting.

Prewiring

There may be times when you need informal discussions with meeting participants before your meeting. Ethan M. Rasiel and Paul Friga termed these one-on-one pre-meetings "prewiring." There are various reasons why this would be beneficial. If you want to ensure the participants arrive fully informed and ready to make a decision, meeting in advance helps you prepare them. You can avoid unpleasant surprises in your meeting by "prewiring" if you'll be addressing a sensitive topic.

You can do this by having conversations or informal meetings one-on-one with participants before your meeting. Situations in which you might wish to do this:

- To have advance discussions with participants to secure buy-in on decisions or plans.

- To have a clear understanding of someone's perspective or concerns before the meeting to avoid surprises.

- To provide supplemental in-depth information before the meeting to be better prepared.

Prewiring can be especially useful if you have someone who you anticipate will challenge items during the meeting. You can address their concerns before the meeting.

You'll have a greater chance of reaching consensus or making decisions if everyone comes to the meeting prepared and ready to move forward.

Another benefit of these conversations is to drum up interest in the meeting and provide reassurance that it will be valuable.

I suggest you approach nay-sayers, one-on-one before you meet with the group so that you can address their concerns in advance of the meeting.

Confirm Access

The suggestion to double check your remote session access might sound obsessive, but I have found myself in the situation more than once when previously scheduled web conference access was not available.

Anne Marie: I did this with my boss before I went on vacation! I had set up executive review sessions (for 270 invitees) under my email, but my boss was going to run the meetings. I wanted to make sure he could open the link and that he could record the session. I was so worried something would go wrong! (It didn't)

This situation happens most often when the meeting is a recurring one. It could be that the number of scheduled reoccurrences completed/expired, or there was a change in the invitation that negatively affected the access number. While this may sound like tedious overkill, take the few minutes needed to confirm your conference access. If you don't take this extra step, you might find yourself in a room full of executives waiting while you try to set up access for those trying to dial in unsuccessfully.

Not a good start.

You never know when this extra step will pay off. Why chance it?

Ask Yourself: Do I have people who will be participating remotely? If so, do I know that the conference access is properly set up?

DURING

The Day of Your Meeting

In addition to leading the meeting, there are other activities you need to carry out to support great results. Many are obvious, but there are details you'll hopefully find helpful to improve your meeting's success.

Printouts

Make sure all needed documents are printed and ready to go well in advance of your meeting. You don't want to stress out over a printer that quit working as you're trying to make those 20 copies only 30 minutes before the meeting. If you want to be extra certain of low-stress meeting preparation, print your documents in advance of your meeting date, such as the day before. This way you arrive at work the day of the meeting with no printing to worry about.

Print the agenda, presentations, and any supporting reference materials that you'll use during the meeting.

Note: You may not need to have printouts if you'll be sharing everything via projector and web access.

<u>Pro Tip</u>: If your meeting is early in the day, make copies the day before the meeting. That way, if you get caught in traffic, or called to an unexpected meeting, or the copy/printer doesn't work, you're still ready to walk into your meeting with all your necessary documents.

Ask Yourself: Do I need to provide printed documentation for this meeting?

Room Setup

Arrive with enough time to set everything up before the planned start time. Aim for having everything ready to go several minutes before the meeting is scheduled to start. You'll be far more at ease if you're all set up and ready as participants arrive.

For example, if your meeting starts at 1:00 pm, then by 12:50 pm aim to have the projector set up, the telephone conference bridge dialed in, and the web conference logged in, so you're available to greet attendees as they arrive. You can then begin the meeting promptly at 1:00 pm.

If you find yourself waiting outside a conference room while a previous meeting is wrapping up, others will understand. You'll be far more relaxed about it if your reputation is one of being well-prepared.

There are situations that will require you to arrive even earlier for your meeting:

If your meeting is being held offsite, you'll need time to prepare the room and address unexpected challenges with an unfamiliar location. If you've forgotten something, you'll have time to call your office to ask someone who is coming to bring the item you may have forgotten. Arriving extra early gives you enough time to attend to the smallest detail and deal with the facility's staff for any last-minute glitches. If everything is set up nice and early, you can relax for the rest of the time before people start arriving.

If you have special setup needs like configuring the meeting space in a certain way or providing working materials, you'll need to arrive early to set up. For example, if you are holding a workshop or training session, and you're providing training books or working materials, allow plenty of time to get there, get the room prepared, lay out the materials the attendees need and have time to relax before their arrival.

Ask Yourself: How much setup time will I need to allow for my meeting?

Running the Meeting

Many meetings lack focus and aren't productive. People stray off-topic, and there are no clear outcomes. By following the steps below, you will run your meeting professionally and efficiently.

Start on Time

Get in the habit of starting your meetings on time. If the culture in your organization is for participants to arrive several minutes after the start time, you'll need to explain, going forward, that you'd like to respect everyone's time and start promptly. If the majority of your attendees are present and ready, start your meeting. It will earn you respect from your peers. People will come to understand that you start your meetings promptly at the listed start time.

Exception: If you're presenting to superiors who have not yet arrived, you'll likely need to wait out of deference. If the meeting is scheduled to start at 1:00 pm and one of the Vice Presidents isn't there yet, simply tell the group that you'll wait for her to arrive. They'll understand. If the Vice President still hasn't arrived at 1:10, yet all other attendees are there, you can ask the group for guidance on how to proceed. "I realize that Jane isn't here yet. Should we wait for her to arrive?" Because they are her peers, they'll have a better sense of the culture, political climate, and the most appropriate way to proceed. One of them may have even received a text saying to go ahead and start the meeting.

Ask Yourself: Am I comfortable setting a standard for punctual start times?

Documenting Attendees

If you have people on the phone or attending remotely, make sure you know who is there. You can ask who is on the call to make sure you've accounted for everyone.

You'll need to include the names of attendees in your meeting notes. It may be necessary for historical purposes. If you are asked later who attended during important decisions, you'll have a record.

Exceptions: There are times when it may not be as important to get the names of all who are present at the start time. Your web access software might provide visibility to know who is attending offsite. Some conference software tools provide reports afterward on who attended the session.

An example of a situation in which you may not need to get the list of attendees at the beginning could be a software demonstration to a large group.

Ask Yourself: Do I need to gather the names of those in attendance at the start of the meeting?

Introductions

If participants don't know one another, allow them to introduce themselves briefly, along with stating their respective relationship to the project. Doing this gives participants context during discussions.

I've held meetings that included participants that I already knew. On these occasions, I often assumed that everyone already knew one another, only to find that I was wrong. It's easy to find out if everyone has previously met. Ask the group. They'll let you know if introductions are needed.

If it's a group of participants you haven't met before, you'll likely want assistance with remembering names during the meeting. I know someone who asks the group to make name plates. She has participants fold an 8 1/2 x 11 piece of paper lengthwise, write their first and last name on both sides and prop it up in front of themselves. She usually says that she's bad at remembering names, especially when she meets a lot of people at once. Both sides are so she can read the name of the person sitting beside her. Papers tend to get moved around during meetings, so it's helpful to have both sides visible.

Ask Yourself: Am I certain all participants know one another already?

Icebreakers

If the group is newly formed and will be working together for a while, icebreakers can help the group quickly build rapport and trust. If you're bringing together two existing teams that worked well independently but not previously together, an icebreaker can facilitate merging the teams.

Note that not every meeting needs ice-breaker activities. In fact, there are times when it's best not to use one. Situations such as the following would not warrant an icebreaker activity:

- If your team is meeting to address an urgent situation or crisis. In this situation, it's time to get down to business and focus on the problem.

- If you're meeting with high-level executives for a formal business meeting, you likely need to stay focused on the meeting topic and not spend time on icebreakers. Executives will have tight schedules and the time is better spent focusing on the business at hand.

Here are a few simple icebreakers that are easy to do:

- **Recommend a great book:** Ask participants to tell about a great book that they would recommend, and why. It not only provides some insight about the individual, but the group will come away with great suggestions.

- **Two lies and a truth:** Have participants share three pieces of information, two of which are lies and one is true. Participants must guess which statement is the true one.

- **Favorite meal:** Have participants tell what their favorite meal is. It could be something they order out or prepare themselves. You'll likely have an engaging discussion about several suggestions, and even recipe requests.

- **Time machine:** Ask participants where they'd go if they could climb aboard a time machine. Which time period would they visit and why?

- **Who is it?** Ask each player to write a fact about themselves that others don't yet know on a notecard. The facilitator collects the cards and reads them aloud. As she reads each one, the group guesses which participant wrote the fact.

Ask Yourself: Is this a new team that needs to build rapport and trust?

If so, with which icebreaker shall we begin?

Meeting Intent

At the start of the meeting, after introductions, remind the group of the meeting goals or intended outcome(s). Decisions or recommendations are needed by the end of the meeting, stating the desired outcome at the start of the gathering helps to drive the meeting toward that result and gets all participants working toward that goal.

The goal needs to be listed on the agenda, and it should be repeated, but it's helpful to give some context around it. Why are you developing a new product? How did we get here? Where are we going and how does our product/decision contribute to the organization's goals? What direction do we have from the executives?

You don't have to spend a lot of time on this, but it can be valuable. If you're on a high-priority project, context around executive support and background helps the team understand why the goal is important. The group can move forward with that in mind.

Ask Yourself: What is the goal or intended outcome of this meeting?

Why is it important?

Follow the Agenda

Because you've made and distributed an agenda with the intended meeting purpose included, everyone should be aware of why you're meeting.

Keep the agenda visible and follow it as closely as possible. It's critical to keep everyone focused, on-topic and to end on time.

There are times when it's valid to allow an agenda item to run long. If you're covering a critical topic and the discussion is valuable—even though it may be running longer than the time allocated on the agenda—you may need to let it go longer. Knowing when to let a topic run long and when to cut it off often requires familiarity with the project and team. If you're not sure, you could ask the group. For instance, *"I realize we're running longer on this topic, but it appears we're making real progress on it and will be able to reach a decision. Should we go a bit longer and work toward a decision during this meeting, or do you think we need to schedule another session for it separately?"*

Ask Yourself: Am I comfortable keeping the group on track following the Agenda?

Facilitate the Discussion

Chairing meetings is a skill that not everyone has naturally, but it can be developed. As the facilitator, you must think on two levels. Everyone else is focused on the content of the discussion, and you will be too. You need to be aware of the time, notice if everyone is contributing, and keep things moving forward. Maintaining the balance of staying on task, yet allowing for a productive level of discussion that doesn't stray too far off topic.

Your job during the meeting is to lead the group through the agenda and work toward completing the meeting goals.

You will need to be engaged and actively managing the group and discussion. There are many things to be aware of during the meeting to keep it moving forward and productive.

I'll go through them below:

Don't dominate the discussion yourself. Your role as facilitator is to get input and guide others in the dialogue. Ask the right questions to generate productive contributions. Frame the scope of the discussion to target your group's focus. For example, remind them what the focus is as well as what it is not.

Encourage participation by attendees. If people don't speak up, you can call them by name and ask if they have anything to add to a topic. You might say something as simple as, "Tom, what's your opinion on this?" or "Janet, we haven't heard from you, and I know that your team has dealt with this recently. You likely have good insight on this. Would you be willing to share?"

If you don't understand a statement made by someone during the meeting, paraphrase or ask for clarification. You want to ensure you and others understand and keep the discussion moving forward. You can even say, "I'm not sure I know what you mean." If there's discussion on a point that isn't clear to everyone, you might offer a summary explanation. Doing so eliminates misunderstanding, so all can participate in the discussion or give informed input.

Watch body language to read reactions. If, during a discussion, someone furrows his brow as if in confusion, feel free to ask if he has questions about the topic. If someone seems in strong disagreement but is not speaking up, you can ask his opinion or concern about an issue.

If a conversation goes on too long, to the point where it's no longer moving forward, or everyone has reached an agreement, it's time to wrap it up and proceed to the next item. Close the discussion when the following situations occur:

- You can't move forward without getting more information outside of the meeting. For example, there's data or information that participants need to make an informed decision.

- You can't move forward until members discuss with others outside the meeting. For example, deciding how to communicate an organizational change might need input from directors.

- You discover that you don't need the entire group for the decision, and it can be settled "offline," outside of the meeting. For example, a decision affects only a small group and doesn't involve most of the attendees.

- Upcoming changes will affect the item you're discussing, so no decisions can be made until the changes occur. You'll need to revisit the decision later. For example, you learn during the meeting that a team will have a substantial reorganization in the next few weeks.

- You need input from people who are not present at the meeting.

- You discover that the topic is too large for the time allotted and you need a separate session dedicated to the decision. You may need to bring the group together for a dedicated working session with whiteboards and longer time to work through it. For example, determining a process for a governance decision.

Ask Yourself: What is one way I can imp
facilitate a meeting?

Bad Me
fa

Respectful Conflict

If the group has been called together to solve a problem, meeting members may express many different ideas and opinions during the discussion. Exploring these different ideas can be valuable and help the group come to a stronger decision.

The key to letting this happen successfully is to follow the discussion and make sure it stays respectful and productive. If things get heated, or it seems that the group cannot reach a decision, it's time to wrap it up and move forward. As the facilitator, you'll need to step in to de-escalate and move the group forward. To do this effectively and respectfully, you can say, "It doesn't appear we'll be able to reach an agreement/decision during this meeting. Let's identify how we can best move forward on it outside of this meeting." If that doesn't feel right to you, some other helpful phrasing in this situation could be the following:

"Karen and Ed, you both make good points. I don't think we'll be able to resolve that discussion during the time we have left."

"It's helpful to hear the different perspectives, but it doesn't seem we'll be able to agree on this. I think we need to move forward with the agenda."

"It seems we may have to agree to disagree."

Sometimes, someone may like their idea so much that when there are different ideas offered, they take it personally. Egos get in the way. During these situations, the group needs a strong

51

cilitator to acknowledge and validate the approach, focus on the pros and cons, and move the conversation forward. This gets easier with practice and experience. Get comfortable with the phrasing suggestions above, or come up with your own. Practice beforehand if you think this type of disagreement will make you uncomfortable. If you find yourself in this situation, you'll be better prepared to address it smoothly.

Ask Yourself: How am I most comfortable dealing with conflict during a meeting?

The "Parking Lot"

Often, meeting attendees raise valuable points during the meeting that aren't on topic with any of the agenda items. A parking lot is a list of these things that you create during the meeting. By documenting this list of off-topic-yet-important points, you can capture them for later follow-up. You can create this list on a whiteboard, on a flip chart, or simply on paper or your laptop if you're using it for capturing notes during the meeting.

You'll likely not have trouble using the parking lot, as it's familiar to many. If it's new to your organization, explain it briefly at the beginning of the meeting. Say that you'll create a parking lot list for items that are off topic, yet still important and need attention.

How to do it: When someone brings up an off-topic subject, acknowledge it and its importance. Let the group know that you'll capture it in the parking lot for later follow-up. At the end of the meeting, read aloud the list of parking lot items, so everyone is confident that you've adequately captured them. If there's a confusing item, ask who you should follow-up with on that particular topic so that you'll know next steps for it.

It is important to take follow-up action on these items. Whether it's having a conversation with the person that brought it up initially, scheduling another meeting to address it specifically, or anything else that may be needed. Otherwise, team members won't trust you to give "parking lot" items any further attention. They'll simply come to see it as a "black hole" and doubt your credibility. You may find that there are parking lot items that need a good deal more attention and could even be opportunities to get face-time with senior executives.

Ask Yourself: Am I prepared to follow up with any parking lot items that may arise in a meeting?

Meeting Notes

During the meeting, write brief notes on items discussed. It can be hard to stay engaged in the discussion and take detailed notes. Keep the notes high-level if possible. Instead of capturing everything said, summarize the main points. You may want to use an easy shorthand to help capture the notes more quickly. Adopting a few commonly used words of shorthand can help. Feel free to make up your own symbols or abbreviations if necessary.

Early in my career, I captured much of the conversation that occurred in meetings. It kept me from being engaged in the discussion itself. Instead, I was more of a transcriber. It resulted in me contributing less to the discussion. I created long meeting notes that no one actually read. I've learned over my career that high-level notes are usually sufficient. Those who were not able to attend can review them much more easily. There have been times when I needed to go back to past meeting notes to find the date of a specific decision. It was much faster to go through high-level notes that have bullet points and summary statements. If someone new comes into the project and wants to review history, they'll be grateful that they can get an easy review of past meetings and decisions.

If possible, get someone else to capture meeting notes. It's much harder to stay engaged with the discussion, read body language, watch the time, move the discussion forward, and write meeting notes all at the same time. Before the meeting, ask someone if they'll take the notes for you. If you have a regularly recurring meeting, you could rotate the role of scribe among the participants.

I've known facilitators who record the meetings and write the notes from the recordings. I've used this approach in the past. I found it to be less efficient since I had to sit through the entire meeting again when listening to the recording.

Ask Yourself: How will I capture meeting notes?

Will I do it myself or have another attendee perform that function?

If I'm responsible for capturing meeting notes, how can I do it most effectively?

Decisions

If the group makes a decision, restate it for clarity. If the decision is not clearly summarized and shared, you may find later that others didn't realize the group had made a decision.

Include the decisions in your meeting notes (explained below). It makes it clear to everyone what the decision was so there's no confusion or disagreement later.

If you're not clear on the final decision made, you can ask for clarification. Simply say "I'm not clear on the decision that was made. Can someone please state it so that I can accurately capture it for our notes and records?" You'll find that others are happy to do so.

Ask Yourself: How will I record decisions made during the meeting?

Action Items

As you identify action items during your meeting, put these in your notes, along with the person responsible and target follow-up or completion dates. If you don't identify an accountable person and an end date, it will most likely not get addressed.

If someone says that they will complete an action item, let them know you expect them to be accountable. Say something like "Great, Cheryl; I have you down for that action item. What target completion date should I set for that?" By doing so, you make it clear that they now own the follow-up. By setting the target completion date themselves, it will be far easier to hold them accountable, and you'll know when to expect it to be finished.

At the end of your meeting, read aloud the list of action items you've captured, those responsible, and the target completion dates. Make sure the action items are easy to spot among your meeting notes so that you don't stumble through reading all your meeting notes to find them. One simple way to handle this in your notes is to tag each with an easy-to-see symbol. Another option is to write them all in a separate section or sheet of paper. The key is to make sure you've captured it clearly and can remind everyone before you adjourn of what they are accountable.

My friend Anne Marie offered this approach:

A technique I learned in my organizational behavior class in grad school is that you're supposed to let the person say her action items out loud rather than reading them back to her. When a person says something out loud in front of other people, it creates a different level of accountability than when someone tells her to do it.

Ask Yourself: How can I remember to capture target due dates and person responsible for action items?

Next Steps

If you're meeting on a topic that will need follow-up activity, talk with the group to confirm next steps. For example, if your group has decided on how to communicate a large change, your next steps might be to talk with the communication coordinator on how to get this information out. Or if you've determined that an additional team needs to be involved in the discussion, next steps will be to schedule a meeting with that team.

Note: These may overlap with action items.

Clearly, identify next steps in your meeting notes, so they don't get buried in the text. Like the action items, you'll read these aloud to remind the group at the end of the meeting.

Ask Yourself: How can I remember to have the group identify our next steps?

Ending the Meeting

Watch the time and don't go longer than scheduled. Your attendees have other commitments, and you need to respect their time. Others may have another meeting that starts as soon as yours ends. You want to have a reputation for ending your meetings on time. If you don't get through all the agenda items, determine if another meeting will be needed or if you can handle the remaining topics via email or some other channel.

If the meeting discussion is still underway with 10 minutes remaining, alert the attendees. You might say, "This is a good discussion. I see that we only have 10 minutes left. Is it possible to come to a decision within that amount of time?"

Note: by putting the most critical or time-sensitive agenda items at the beginning of the meeting, you're sure to address them if the discussion goes long.

There's nothing wrong with ending the session early if you've accomplished the meeting goal. I'm not suggesting rushing things that need adequate discussion, but don't drag things out to fill the entire scheduled meeting time.

If you happen to get through the agenda before the scheduled meeting time has completed, go ahead and adjourn. If you have a suspicion that you might finish before the allotted time, you can say at the beginning of the meeting, "This might not take the entire hour. If so, we can end earlier." Your co-workers will appreciate you for it. My brother-in-law often gets praise from his colleagues for being so efficient that his meetings usually end early.

Ask Yourself: How will I ensure that we end on time if discussions are running long?

Recapping Decisions, Action Items, and Next Steps

Before your meeting adjourns, quickly restate the decisions made, the next steps and the action items, the person responsible, and the due date for follow-up or completion. Don't forget to recap parking lot items.

Because you've made these points easy to spot in your notes, this will be quick and easy to do. Everyone will leave the meeting clear on their respective responsibilities and target due dates. It will give the attendees a sense of accomplishment for their time spent with you, and confidence in you as the facilitator.

Ask Yourself: How will I easily capture and identify decisions, action items and next steps to remind attendees at the end of the meeting?

AFTER

Wrap up

After your successful meeting, you still have several activities to do to ensure you don't lose the value gained in your meeting. These post-meeting activities will make sure that your effort continues to pay off in real value.

Prepare the Meeting Notes

Type and distribute your meeting notes as soon as possible after the meeting. This allows attendees to provide input if any changes are needed. It reduces the risk of not being able to read your quickly written notes or the context of the information. In your meeting notes, include information regarding meeting date, time, location, and attendees.

If your team uses a common document storage repository, upload the file there for historical purposes, so it will be easy to locate if needed.

Include action items and decisions made during the meeting, along with any other critical pieces of information, such as next steps, issues, or parking lot items.

The meeting notes are not formal meeting minutes, but rather a high-level summary and a list of what the group addressed, decisions, follow-up items, and next steps.

Ask Yourself: How soon after the meeting will I type up the notes?

To see templates and samples for these documents be sure to check out the Appendix.

Distributing the Meeting Notes

Send the meeting notes (including the action items and next steps) to all meeting invitees, whether they attended or not. If someone was unable to attend, the meeting notes will inform them of discussion points and decisions.

Ask for any modifications that might be needed. You could call them "draft meeting notes" and ask for feedback/corrections within two days. If someone suggests a revision, update the draft notes. Then after the 2-day time period, the notes are official and can be distributed to all attendees. If no corrections or changes are made, the notes do not need to be redistributed.

When I send the meeting notes, I usually include a list of the action items in the body of the email. I include this information in the meeting note document, but I find that often people don't read the meeting notes. If you have listed the action items along with the person responsible in the body of your email, it ensures everyone is reminded. This additional step increases visibility and accountability.

Ask Yourself: Will I send meeting notes within 24 hours after the meeting?

Follow-Up on Post Meeting Commitments

Action Items and Commitments. Simply compiling a list of action items during your meeting doesn't ensure that those responsible will carry them out. They may have good intentions during the meeting. However, people get busy and distracted with other work. They may have forgotten about their tasks in the midst of other activities.

Follow up one-on-one with each person responsible for action items.

Don't wait until the due date. A few days before the deadline, send a short email asking about the status of the item. The reminder allows time to still complete the item by the deadline. Assume positive intent and reach out in a positive way.

If you are the one who is expected to keep up with the action items, as well as status, you'll benefit from setting up some form of a tracking system. Creating a task log can help. There are various tools you could use for this, so use the one that's most comfortable and easy to use. Microsoft Excel or some other spreadsheet-type tool can be easily formatted to track tasks, those responsible, and status.

Parking Lot Items. Don't forget about the parking lot items. You committed to follow up on these, so keep your word. Take appropriate action as needed, whether it's scheduling a separate meeting or following up with someone one-on-one for information.

Ask Yourself: How will I keep track of action items, commitments, and parking lot items?

Feedback

If you want to know what went well and what you could improve, ask for feedback from someone who attended the meeting and who you trust to give you honest feedback. Let him know that you want to improve your performance and ensure that the meetings are productive for the team. Ask specific questions. If the feedback needs more clarification, ask him to elaborate.

Afterward, be sure to thank this person who has given you feedback. Let him know that you appreciate his time and willingness to be open with you. Make an honest effort to incorporate the suggestions going forward. And you may want to let him know if you had success with a proposal. He'll appreciate that you took the advice to heart.

Ask Yourself: Whom can I trust to give me honest, constructive feedback?

Action Items

Now that you've captured the action items from your meeting make sure that you can track them easily. If the meeting is for an ongoing project that you lead, keep up with the status of the action items. An "Action Item Log" can help. Your team may have a tool already in place that you can use. If not, an Excel spreadsheet works well.

ACTION ITEM LOG

Project Name: Genesis Project

ID	Action Item	Owner	Due Date	Priority	Comments	Closed Date

See examples on the next page.

ACTION ITEM LOG

Project Name: Genesis Project

ID	Action Item	Owner	Due Date	Priority	Comments	Closed Date
1	Send last status to Wayne W.	Sam Phillips	03/05/18	Low		03/04/18
2	Finalize Chuck Elliott's teams	Sam Phillips	03/20/18	Medium	Get final confirmation from Chuck	
3	Contact server team for project needs	Vienna Teng	03/25/18	High	Contact Sharon Keener	
4	Confirm license quantity	Amy Langston	04/13/18	High	Need contact names for various areas	

Finish this sentence: I can create an Action Item Log using _____.

Checklists, templates and samples are located in the Appendix at the end of this book. Additionally, these materials can be downloaded by visiting the following link:

https://www.projectbliss.net/greatmeetings/

PART 2:

BOOSTING YOUR IMPACT

OTHER COMPONENTS OF A SUCCESSFUL MEETING

Part one of this book deals with all the activities needed for planning and executing your successful meeting.

The second part gives you tools to achieve the best outcome. It identifies common challenges and ways to work around them.

The following items can positively affect the quality and success of your meeting.

- Identifying what approach to use, based on the type of meeting you're leading, can help you get the most out of your session.

- Knowing common challenges, you may face and how to deal with them can help you navigate them smoothly with grace and poise.

- Using the right seating layout to ensure the best communication for your meeting goals.

"Make the best use of what is in your power, and take the rest as it happens."
Epictetus

TYPES OF MEETINGS—IN DEPTH

The focus of this book is on making meetings productive. To do so, it's helpful to understand the different types of meetings and the special needs of each. I've broken them down into several categories and provide information about each of the following:

- Problem-solving meeting

- Decision-making

- Brainstorming / Innovation

- Information Sharing

- Status Update

- Other

Note: There may be overlap or a combination of two or more types of meetings.

Problem-Solving Meetings

Objective

In problem-solving meetings, you and your team work to devise a viable solution to a problem. You'll seek a solution that's feasible with respect to financial constraints and can be completed within the preferred time frame.

Approach

Depending on the scope and complexity of the issue the group must deal with, as well as how quickly the solution needs to be implemented, problem solving could be conducted in one session or might take several. With the appropriate people at the table, the team may be able to present information, address it and devise a solution in with only one meeting. For example, selecting a location for a team outing could be done in only one meeting if you have all the relevant players present and the necessary information on which to base your decision.

If the problem is large and has a broader impact, several sessions might be needed. If the group seeks to create a new process, more meetings over the course of several weeks or months likely would be necessary.

Listed below are the standard steps to use when solving a problem.

- **Define the Problem.** This is the background information that gives all participants the who, what, where, why and when. They need to have a clear understanding of what the situation is, who it affects, the location of the issue, why it causes roadblocks, and when the challenge occurs. Answer additional questions to fill in knowledge gaps for the group.

- **Analyze the problem.** Once you've identified the problem, evaluate it further to determine if more information is needed or if you've identified the actual problem. There may be a root cause that you've not considered. I've provided several tools for this in this section under "Problem Solving Tools."

- **Identify requirements and constraints.** It's important to know the requirements and limitations your team is working within. For example, you might need to complete work more quickly, but you won't be able to hire additional resources. Maybe your software needs to use a specific language, or the constraint might be that the solution must be available within a specific time window. The group must agree on and prioritize the important solution criteria. These can vary according to the group's needs, such as immediacy, cost, and long-term benefit.

Example:

Your team is trying to figure out how to train the end users for a new software application you'll be rolling out. You want to give your end-users a positive experience from the get-go, but some approaches will be expensive and ultimately, cost prohibitive. Some approaches will take longer. If you fly your team to different end user locations to train face-to-face, this will be costly and slow. Putting training documents online will be faster, but won't give the end user the high-touch service you'd like to provide.

- **The team needs to decide which criteria are most important:** speed, cost, or the value of the face-to-face experience. They need to be clear on what's not an option due to constraints. It might be that the budget won't cover the cost of travel. This will help your team make the decision that best fits the situation.

- **Brainstorm possible solutions**. Encourage the group to propose all possible solutions and don't criticize any ideas. Allow all options to be considered to keep creativity and ideas flowing. (Brainstorming guidelines are provided more thoroughly in the "Brainstorming meeting" section in this chapter.)

Example:

If you're brainstorming training solutions and Gary suggests hiring a vendor to deliver the training, don't judge the suggestion as too expensive or not an option. It will cause others to be cautious about making suggestions. Brainstorming is about getting all ideas out there before judging them.

- **Evaluate best potential solutions.** Once the group has generated a list of possible ideas, identify the best possible solutions for more discussion and evaluation. Examine how they might satisfy the need or affect the organization. What are the benefits and downsides of each? Look at factors such as implementation cost and complexity, timeline, and quality. Question the pros and cons of each option. Which option can most realistically be implemented? What impediments would prevent you from implementing particular solutions?

Example:

Many ideas were generated through brainstorming solution ideas for training. The group now selects the best options from the list.

Flying team members out to different division sites will be too expensive to do right now, so they put that idea aside. Shannon really likes the idea of offering face-to-face on-site training. The group suggests that if a division decides it is important enough to them, the division might pay for the travel. The team keeps this option open if that situation comes up.

The team decides that creating short videos to put online are cost effective and give the users a clear idea of how to use the software. The documentation is inexpensive and can be created easily by the team. This is the team's preferred solution.

- **Agree on the choice** Once the group has discussed the options, shared opinions, and explored each more thoroughly, decide which solution to choose. All involved in the meeting should have an opportunity to give input and share their opinions. Everyone should have the same understanding of what the final decision is and agree that this was the best option.

Example:

The group identifies that short online videos and documents explaining how to use the software are the best approaches. They clearly state the final decision and record it for the meeting notes. Everyone agrees that this is the decision that has been made.

In an ideal world, everyone would happily agree on a final determination. There would be complete consensus on the best option. This is not always the case. In situations where the group is not in agreement on the final decision, there are several decision-making approaches that the group could take. A variety of approaches are provided in the "Decision-Making Meetings" section of this book.

Challenges

Participants. In your meeting, include people affected by the problem or the resulting change.

The scope of the problem will determine who your meeting participants are. If your issue affects many different areas, you may want representation from those areas. If the problem affects a large organization, choose representatives from affected areas who understand the problem, possess historical knowledge and can communicate well with their respective teams. This will help the group make more informed decisions.

For example, if you're trying to solve the problem of low community usage for a local playground, include park maintenance in your discussion. In addition, you'll want to include representation from local parents. They'll be able to give insight you may not have considered.

71

- **Facilitator**. You, as the facilitator, should understand how to run this type of meeting productively and use tools and processes that produce constructive results. It's best if you are neutral on the outcome. You don't want to direct the conversation toward one solution over another. The goal is to have the group come up with the solution that best fits the needs of all involved.

- **Large problems.** Break large problems down into smaller components. Rather than let the complexity and size overwhelm you, use the problem-solving tools provided in this section to guide you to a productive solution.

Tools

Problem solving on its own could be a book in itself. I want to give you several tools so you can immediately start addressing current issues. Here are five popular problem-solving approaches. They are appreciation, root cause analysis, Five Whys, drill down and cause and effect.

➢ **Appreciation:** This technique was developed by the military to help identify the best course of action to take in a specific situation. It can easily be applied to business.

To carry out this exercise, the team identifies the problem and then asks, "So what?" Another statement will be made as an inference or deduction from the original problem statement. You then again ask "So what?" and so on until you get to an area that's beneficial to address.

You can do this exercise multiple times with the same problem statement and follow several different paths.

Example: You own a grocery business, and the power is out.

Situation: The power is out.

So what? Food will spoil.

So what? We're losing money.

Situation: The power is out.

So what? Food will spoil.

So what? We'll need staff to come in and remove the lost inventory.

So what? We'll need to let them know now and schedule them for it. We'll need to have a plan to dispose of all this waste.

Situation: The power is out.

So what? Security system is down.

So what? We'll need to plan for backup security.

You can continue in various ways to identify multiple paths or courses of action.

This approach helps you fully understand the impact of a problem. You'll get more clarity on where to place focus and the effects of the issue you've identified. As a result, you'll uncover potential courses of action you may not have thought of otherwise. It's a simple and straightforward way to examine a problem. Note that in this context, the word appreciation could be defined as evaluation.

➢ **Root Cause Analysis:** Look at what caused the problem to occur so that you can address the root and prevent the problem from happening again.

Root causes tend to fit into three categories.

- **Physical:** a tangible, material item has failed to perform in the expected and intended manner.

- **Human:** some type of human behavior caused the problem. Human causes can lead to physical causes. For example, if a human does not replace seals on a machine, it can cause the machine to malfunction.

- **Organizational:** a faulty process or policy. For example, if there is no accountability for carrying out actions, this could lead to lack of individuals taking responsibility.

To use this approach, ask three questions. What happened? Why did it happen? And, how can we keep it from happening again?

Example: You own a grocery business, and you're losing refrigerated inventory due to a power outage.

Situation: Our refrigerated inventory is spoiling due to lack of refrigeration.

What happened? We lost power during the storm.

Why did it happen? Lightning struck the transformer, and we lost power.

How can we keep it from happening again? We could purchase a generator or alternate power source as a backup for emergencies.

- ➢ **Five Whys:** Continue to ask "why" until you get to the root of the problem. Five Whys might not be best for large and especially, complex problems. It can be good for simple ones. As it is a relatively simple approach, it's worth giving a try. It can be combined with other tools.

To carry out the Five Whys activity, state the problem, then ask "Why?" Come up with a valid answer for why the problem occurred. Write this reason next to your "why" question. Then for that reason, again ask "Why?" Continue to ask "why" until you get to a reason that can be addressed. You may not need to ask "Why" exactly five times. This number is only a guideline. Make sure you don't stop too soon, though.

Example: Executive reports were not compiled as needed.

Situation: Our team didn't meet the deadline for running executive reports.

Why? There was no one ready to run the reports in time.

Why? The person who usually runs the executive reports was on vacation, so there was no one ready to run them.

Why? There was no backup in place for that activity.

Why? Because none had been identified.

This might be enough for your team to work with the solution.

Another example:

Situation: One of our machines is not working.

Why? We discovered that there are loose connections.

Why? They were loosened by constant vibration from the heavier machinery nearby.

Why? The heavier machine was not properly anchored down.

Here we realize that the adjacent machine needs proper anchoring.

Team missed the deadline for running executive reports.

WHY?

No one was onsite to run the reports.

WHY?

Person who regularly runs reports was on vacation so no one was onsite to do the job.

WHY?

No backup in place for that activity.

WHY?

No one had been identified as the backup to run reports.

➤ **Drill Down:** Break a problem down into smaller pieces that the team can then address. This can be good for larger, more complex problems. It helps break them into smaller components that can then each be addressed individually.

Write down the main problem. Next, to it, write down smaller points or issues that make up the problem. These should be one level down from the main issue. You're breaking it down one level, rather than many micro-level issues. For each of these components, keep breaking each part down further. Continue working your way down another level deeper until you can't drill down further. At this point, you can start looking for solutions to these bottom layer items.

If you need more information about any of these paths, carry out any research your team needs. Identify if and where the group needs to follow up to gather more data. This is a great opportunity to delegate tasks and list them as follow-up items on your meeting notes with the assigned person's name and corresponding due date.

This process will help you uncover items you hadn't considered and will give you a deeper understanding of the issue. You'll get clarity to contributing factors you may not have seen. Some elements may need further investigation or research to be able to solve the problem. This process works well with the "Five Whys" Technique.

An example: Class grades have been falling over the past year. This problem can be broken down into multiple components that can each be examined and addressed.

We could look at environmental factors, such as on-site construction that's causing distracting noise. We may identify lower parental involvement this year.

We'd want to drill down further and examine why parental involvement has dropped and how to increase it. High absentee rate due to a larger-than-normal flu outbreak might be added to the list. This might inspire the school administration to promote a vaccination campaign next year. We could continue to break these down further as needed.

Another example could be low software adoption rates. We can break this down into multiple components and decide what to address.

We learn from an employee in one department that the rollout team didn't communicate broadly on the software changes. Some of the staff who were absent on the day of the rollout never received communication that a change was happening. We can determine how to address that issue in various ways.

Moving forward, we can consider if it's better to focus on increasing adoption based on physical locations or VP groups.

We decide that it is more cost effective to increase adoption based on physical location. Based on that, we consider holding training sessions at each location. This is a viable option if we hold multiple, small group meetings, so as not to tie up all the staff at one time.

We could break this area down further in to Help Desk support and Training. We can then develop a strategy for each of these areas to improve user experience and increase adoption rates.

An example drill down chart based on this situation is provided below.

Problem: Low adoption rates for new software

Communication
- Presentations ——→ Determine locations / teams
- Website ——→ Need strategy
- Email campaign ——→ Need strategy

Rollout strategy ——→ Business groups v location

User experience
- Help Desk Support
    - Help desk staff ——→ Help desk staff needs more training

    - Users
        o Post contact information in multiple locations
        o Remind users to open help tickets rather than calling developers

- Training
    - Training materials
        o Post user guides on site for easy access
        o Record webinars
        o Host Q & A sessions

    - On-site training for remote locations ——→ How to cover travel costs?

➢ **Cause and Effect Diagram (Fishbone):** In this technique, you explore all the possible sources of the problem. This approach gives visibility to the various base causes and shows you where to focus your efforts.

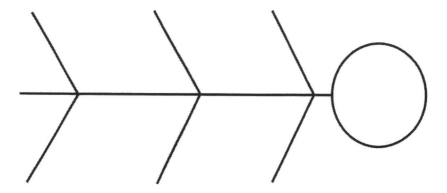

This technique uses a tool called a Fishbone diagram because the finished graphic looks like the bones of a fish. It's referred to as Ishikawa Diagram. Kaoru Ishikawa devised it in the 1960s and published in his book *Introduction to Quality Control.*

Write the problem in a box or circle on the side of a piece of paper or whiteboard. From this box, draw a horizontal line. You'll write ideas and possible causes from this line. Identify different categories to address when looking at possible reasons for the current issue.

To give insight into various ways to break it out, Ishikawa identified the following categories for examination. These are known as the 6 M's., or the 5 M's. and 1 P. They are:

- Method

- Mother Nature (Environmental)

- Man (People)

- Measurement

- Machine

- Materials

Modify the categories to fit your needs. If you work in marketing, for example, you could to use the 4 P's of Marketing (Product, Place, Price, and Promotion) for your categories.

Example: The business can't accommodate all t-shirt orders.

Draw the diagram with the problem statement and each of the categories.

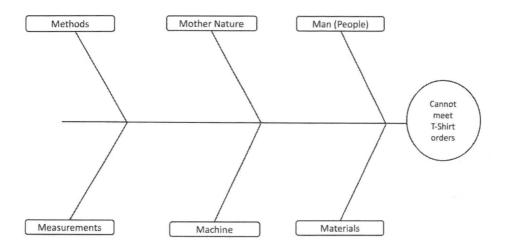

Next, identify possible problem areas in each category.

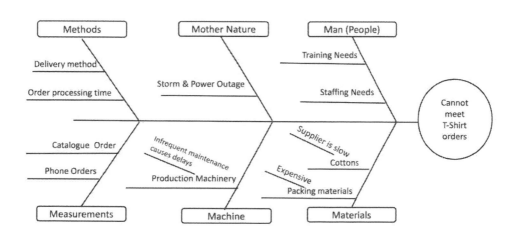

The diagram will begin to look like this:
Within each of these areas, identify possible issues.

You'll likely find more than you can address at once. Assess the areas and identified opportunities. You don't have to tackle everything at the same time.

The group can determine where to focus first for the biggest return. Make sure to document this information. It will be valuable in the future, in case your team wants to address other problem areas later.

If your problem is complex with serious impacts, it can be helpful to bring in a facilitator skilled in problem-solving techniques. For simpler problems, you can do these without additional help. If you have further interest, research problem-solving techniques such as Six Sigma tools.

Decision-Making Meetings

Objective

The objective of the decision-making meeting is for the group to reach a conclusion about a specific issue. The final say may need to come from one person or can be made collectively. Either way, the goal is to come away with a clear answer.

Decision-making meetings can be helpful on a variety of issues, ranging from simple to complex. When meeting participants are involved in the decision-making process, they feel more buy-in.

Planning meetings often come under the category of decision-making meetings, as planning can often include making multiple decisions.

When meeting participants are involved in the decision-making process, they feel more buy-in and ownership of the decision that's been made.

Approach

Though the goal of the decision-making meeting is to reach a resolution, there are several ways it can be made:

- By one person or a few people, usually the senior members of the group with more authority.

- By a team empowered to make the decision.

- By a unanimous agreement of all members of the group (this can be the most difficult to achieve).

If the decision needs to be made by executives, you'll need to ensure that relevant data and key participants are at your meeting. Invite people who can answer key questions and provide information to enable the executives to make an informed decision.

If the conclusion will be made by peers or a group who needs to come together to come to an agreement, there are several approaches you can take. See the section below on consensus-building techniques.

Make sure all participants have a clear understanding of the scope and end goals of what's being decided. Ensure they have enough lead time to review this information before the meeting by sending it out early.

The group will need relevant background data and information on how the decision might affect the organization. It may be helpful to know why the decision needs to be made. Understanding the impact to the organization and the value to the team will provide context for the group.

For example, you want the group to decide which software feature to add next. Before the meeting, you send out an agenda, which lists this goal above the agenda bullet items. In your accompanying email, you explain the importance of this decision. You share that the group's IT director is scheduled to present the software roadmap at the next VP meeting. She needs a commitment from the team that they can meet the targeted milestones so that she can prepare her presentation.

Provide enough lead time for the participants to process the information before the decision-making meeting. They need to know in advance that the goal for the meeting is to make a decision and what their role is in this session. Planning and preparation are valuable to ensure that the meeting time is well spent. You'll be more likely to reach a decision if everyone comes informed.

It will serve you well as the facilitator to make sure everyone has the same understanding of what's needed, has the

84

necessary information and knows that they need to come to the meeting ready to make a decision. Don't wait until the meeting to inform the participants of this expectation. Give them time to process and think about the problem. They may reach out to you before the meeting to ask questions. If you get the same questions multiple times, use this as an indicator to provide more information.

As the facilitator, it's not your job to influence the decision. If you have a bias, yet want to get an unbiased, true group decision, allow the participants to give all their input and share their opinions. Don't give favor to one viewpoint over another. Allow and encourage all to have their say.

To keep everyone on task, it's imperative to guide the discussion and the decision-making process.

Make sure you have the right people involved. Find out if you need representation from specific areas or if certain decision makers need to be present. Question this beforehand to make sure you don't arrive at the meeting only to find out a key participant is missing.

Some helpful questions to ask in preparation for your meeting:

- Who should be included?

- Are there company guidelines or policies that need to be considered when making this decision?

- Are there industry requirements to keep in mind?

- Who is affected by the problem?

- Who influences the decision? Are there team members who have been vocal in the past on this topic or can have an impact on the decision-maker? Are there team members who might try to negatively influence any decisions?

Determine how to either gain their support or plan for any counter-attack from them. (See the section on prewiring.)

- Who has supporting or important information to help in making this decision?

- Remember that the more people you include in the meeting, the harder it will likely be to reach a decision. Don't include people who don't need to be there or the meeting could become unproductive.

Some helpful items to consider after the meeting is over:

- If participants have follow-up actions or responsibilities after the decision has been made, make sure everyone knows what their responsibilities are. For example, if someone needs to convey information to a larger group confirm that they know they are accountable and will follow through.

- Clearly document decisions made for historical purposes so that you don't find yourself repeating the same process later. Many years ago I worked with a team who agreed to import data manually during a software transition. One of the key participants left the team for another job. The decision hadn't been documented, and the group found itself churning on this discussion once again, with disagreements about how the data transfers would be handled. If the original decision had been documented and shared among all, this could have been avoided.

- Once a decision is made, be clear on next steps and who is responsible for carrying them out. Even if you get your decision, it doesn't do the team any good if the intended actions aren't carried out.

Special considerations for decision-making meetings:

- Make sure that everyone understands you're working toward a decision.

- Make sure that everyone understands the process and tools you'll be using in the session.

- Allow enough time for discussing the problem. Don't rush the discussion or participants won't feel that they were given enough opportunity to explore and give the attention needed to the problem.

- Allow conflict and discussion of different viewpoints. Make sure the group discusses respectfully. Pay attention to both verbal and non-verbal cues to know if discussion gets heated so you can direct it appropriately. Don't shut down disagreements. You want team members to share various perspectives.

- When a decision is made, restate it for clarity. This ensures that you understood correctly. It signals to the group that a final decision was made and what it is.

- Sometimes the conversation can churn, with no progress. If people keep making the same comments over and over and there's no movement forward, confront the group about it. Help the group move the discussion forward toward reaching a decision. Ask why the group can't move forward on making a decision. Do they need more information? What roadblocks do they see in reaching a solution?

- If there are attendees who are not contributing to the discussion, ask them for their input and opinions on the topic.

- Watch body language and question people if they seem to have strong reactions but are not speaking up. If not, you may find that they will present roadblocks after the decision is made. If someone has concerns but doesn't share them in the meeting, this nervousness will surface later. It's easier to deal with unease in the meeting rather than afterward.

- Use problem-solving tools if necessary, such as those listed in the Problem-Solving section.

Challenges

- **Unprepared attendees**. People could come to the meeting without enough information to decide. The meeting turns into an information-sharing session instead, and the group spends the entire time discussing the situation and leaves without making a clear decision. This results in the need to meet again to decide or to conduct more research.

  Make sure that participants/decision-makers have all the information they need ahead of time. This may require having huddles or discussions before the meeting (see the section on prewiring).

  Make sure that everyone knows that the goal of the meeting is to make a decision.

  Send out agendas well in advance. Agendas should clearly state that the meeting goal is to make a decision on the target item.

- **Decision requires consensus.** Getting agreement from all participants is usually difficult. Your situation might require it.

An example from a company where input from all involved is critical.

Anita, who works for a global company based in the United States, was in a problem-solving meeting involving attendees from various countries. They were making changes to a company process. After much debate, one of the attendees from a different country asked, "Why are we spending so much time working on this? Why don't the executives just make a decision and tell everyone how to do it?" Anita explained that that approach doesn't really work well in her country's culture.

Consensus-based decisions are more time consuming and difficult in the short-term, but it might be the approach necessary for your situation. In your organization or situation, it might be important that everyone has an equal chance to affect the outcome to get buy-in and participation from all. Consensus decisions are best used to have strong buy-in and support of the whole group. Full acceptance and cooperation for the final decision can be worth the effort.

Agreement by consensus means that everyone agrees with the decision. They may not all be raving fans of the final choice, but they all agree to go along with the selection. Consensus is reached not by threat or intimidation, but by collaboration and cooperation. Consensus among the group means that the group finds an option that everyone can support. Gaining consensus involves discussing ideas and opinions, understanding that there may be compromise and not getting everything you want.

If it's critical that you gain unanimity, understand that the process may be more difficult or time-consuming. There are several approaches to take to help a group reach agreement when it appears it may be more challenging.

To get consensus, it's not critical that everyone is equally enthusiastic, but that they do agree to go along with the decision. They may not fully agree that it's the best choice, but they realize it is the best choice.

Tools

There are several consensus-building techniques your group could use.

➤ **The Quaker Model:** The Quakers have used a consensus-based decision-making model for many years. It emphasizes listening and sharing information among participants. The model demonstrates mutual respect for other participants and seeks the best outcome for the group rather than for individuals. Everyone gets a chance to speak and share their opinions. No one dominates the discussion. A facilitator makes sure the discussion flows toward a consensus, and everyone can see how the discussion moves in that direction. The decisions that are made are owned by the entire group rather than by only one or a few individuals.

➤ **Consensus-Oriented Decision-Making (CODM):** Tim Hartnett created this step-by-step approach. He defines it in his book Consensus-Oriented Decision-Making: The CODM Model for Facilitating Groups to Widespread Agreement.

This process fosters collective ownership of group decisions. The framework consists of the following seven steps:

• **Frame the topic/problem.** Identify the problem and make sure that the right people are involved in the discussion. Determine the required level of agreement needed to make the decision, such as unanimous, group majority agreement, or executive committee.

- **Have an open discussion**. The group generates and shares ideas about the problem. Don't try to solve the problem yet. Simply gather ideas at this stage.

- **Identify underlying concerns**. The group will likely uncover problems that were not identified initially. Be open to discussing these problems, as they'll help you in making the final decision. The group shouldn't take any of the discussion personally. As the facilitator, keep the discussion respectful and moving forward.

- **Develop proposals.** Review the information the group compiled in the previous steps. Use it to develop more detailed proposals and potential solutions to the identified problems. You may find that components of various suggestions can work together to form a more comprehensive plan.

- **Choose a direction**. Go through each proposal. Decide on the best choice. It could be a combination of more than one option.

- **Develop a preferred solution**. Work with the group to improve the decision where possible. Address outstanding concerns.

- **Closure**. Follow the decision rule your group defined in step one to make certain there is consensus to proceed with the decision.

Voting Techniques

When the group needs to make a final vote, you need to know how you'll carry out the final decision-making. There are various voting techniques that can be used. The following are common options.

- **Majority voting.** Have group members vote on the preferred options. If the situation is sensitive or political, you may prefer anonymity in the voting. You can have participants write their answers on a piece of paper if all are present or you can use online tools and polls that allow for anonymity.

- **Ranking.** To understand how options compare to one another, using a ranking method could be a good choice. The group members each individually record their preferences in rank order. The lead then collects all the individual rankings and adds them together.

For example, if there are five options, each group member writes down their preference in order from favorite to least favorite from one to five, with five being the best. Then each of the items are grouped together with the score of their ranking. They are all ranked together. The one with the highest score wins.

To illustrate, I'll use a simple example. Let's say you have a group of kids who need to select an animal as their team mascot. The group narrows it down to five animals: goldfish, hamster, cat, dog, and pony. To make the final selection, they are then asked a to rank them in order of preference.

Team Mascot Voting

	Gracie	Emery	Sophia	Lucian	Totals
Goldfish	4	1	2	1	8
Hamster	3	2	3	2	10
Cat	5	3	5	5	18
Dog	1	4	4	4	13
Pony	2	5	1	3	11

The kids rank them as such:

After ranking and scoring, we can see that the group has collectively ranked Cat the highest. The cat was selected as the team mascot.

- **Scoring**. This option can be helpful when you want insight to several criteria on which you'll base your decision. This involves identifying the important criteria and then giving a score to each of the criteria. If your team determines that certain criteria are more important than others, you can weight the criteria.

  For example, if your team is trying to decide which supplier to use for a project, you might use the criteria of price, quality, and lead time for delivery. If your team determines that quality is more important than price or lead time, you can give more points to vendors whose products are higher quality.

- **Multiple votes and rounds**. This technique is useful when there are many options, and you want to identify the most popular in a large group. Participants can vote for more than one option in the first voting round. The most popular options go on to the next round, with the least popular options being eliminated. Then another round of voting is held among these remaining options.

An example of how this works: Your team is voting on the next offsite team-building activity. Your boss has asked for a list of ideas from the group. The group collectively suggests bowling, a painting class, a movie, happy hour after work, a climbing wall, a cooking class, a river boat ride, a baseball game, participating in a volunteer activity, and a ropes course.

The group is given the opportunity to vote on all their favorites. Each person can vote for all that are appealing.

The team votes as follows:

Tom:
bowling
happy hour
baseball game
volunteer activity

Sally:
bowling
painting class
happy hour
cooking class
baseball game

Erica:
bowling
happy hour
cooking class
river boat ride

baseball game
volunteer activity
ropes course

<u>Nick:</u>
bowling
painting class
movie
cooking class
baseball game
volunteer activity

<u>Results:</u>
bowling - 4
baseball game - 4
volunteer activity - 3
happy hour - 3
cooking class - 3
painting class-2
movie - 1
river boat ride - 1
ropes course - 1
climbing wall – 0

From the results, we can see that each person had suggested both bowling and baseball. Because the group is small, and two items received unanimous votes from everyone, the boss then tells the group members to each vote between bowling or attending a baseball game. Everyone then votes for bowling.

If the group were larger, they could have decided to vote for everything that received three or more votes.

There can be overlap among the decision-making and problem-solving type meetings. Use problem-solving tools if needed. If you'll be using a tool to solve the problem, make sure that participants understand how to use that tool. Some problem-solving tools that can be used are mentioned in the problem-solving meeting section.

Consensus decisions are best for strong buy-in and whole group support. Full acceptance and cooperation are worth the effort.

Brainstorming/Innovation Meetings

Objective

The purpose of a brainstorming meeting is to generate many new ideas fast. Your group can come up with new ideas or approaches more quickly than one person doing it on their own.

Approach

Identify the team members (or representatives) who may be involved or affected by the decision. If any special expertise is needed, include those subject matter experts. For the best results, include participants who can bring multiple perspectives to the table. By including multiple team members, you can generate ideas that you likely wouldn't with just one or two people, and the team will feel more ownership of the outcome.

If you need certain stakeholder support, include those persons. If they are part of the idea generation and decision-making process, they'll have more buy-in and provide greater support.

Have a note taker capture information. If there are questions about how the decision was made, this will be valuable. If the first choice doesn't work out for some reason, your team can then move to the second choice without having to go through the exercise all over again.

Allow for the team to freely share without the fear of judgment. Create an atmosphere that allows free-flowing ideas. Don't make the structure rigid or too controlled. Allow spontaneous sharing and permit ideas to build.

General approach:

- **Establish guidelines and determine the approach** you'll use with the group. It's helpful if everyone understands how you'll proceed. For example, if you'll use a brainstorming session first, make sure that everyone knows the guidelines.

- **Propose the issue or problem**. Ask participants to share ideas. The key is that no one judges them initially. Everything is an acceptable option. Though some ideas may be impossible, the creativity will inspire more possible solutions.

- **Write the problem statement out** so that it can be clearly considered. For example, "The project budget won't support printing our training materials." This allows your group to look at multiple components of the problem statement. You can see different parts of the problem separately. You can inspect the project budget as well as printing of training materials. It might be that the funding could come from elsewhere, or the training information could be provided electronically.

- **As ideas are generated, other ideas may be inspired.** The more ideas you get, the greater the chance of coming up with great ones. Keep going and allow everything as an option at this point.

- Some people think best in a **quiet space** with time for generating ideas. It can be helpful to give out the assignment well before the meeting and ask participants to be ready to share their ideas when you come together. If there are dominant personalities present, those who think best alone can come with their ideas already prepared.

- Once a list of ideas is generated, use a technique to **scale back the list** of ideas to a shorter selection. You can use ranking or voting, for example, to pare down the options.

- From the pared-down list, **discuss and evaluate each idea.** The group can rank order the suggestions and select the top choice.

The group then determines the next steps and how to implement the idea.

Challenges

- **Ideas judged as they are shared.** Because the intent is to generate ideas if people's ideas are negatively judged then participants will be less likely to share freely. Remind participants that this is a brainstorming activity and everything is acceptable initially.

- **Too many people with little structure.** If you're working with a large group, break them into smaller groups. This allows for more participant involvement within the small groups. Then you can bring each of the groups together to share their ideas with the whole group.

- **Not enough time.** Allow time for ideas to be generated and to follow through with discussions. If you're working with a complex problem, you may need to schedule a longer session.

- **Judgment.** If you work in an environment where there's little trust, attendees may be less open to giving input. Sharing ideas anonymously can be a way to encourage more participation. Use methods that allow team members to share without their names attached to the ideas, such as writing ideas on notecards and putting them in an envelope. This may only be needed in extreme cases, but it's an option if necessary.

- **Poor environment for stimulating creative thinking**. Meet in a different location to inspire new ideas. Ensure there's a way to easily capture and share ideas as they arise. You may want to be in a place where you can move around easily or use a whiteboard to draw or write for all to see. It can be helpful to start the meeting with an activity to stimulate creative thinking. Simple ideas include drawing, creating a sculpture with pipe cleaners or other materials, making paper airplanes, or writing a haiku.

- **No follow-through**. Determine what you'll do next with these ideas. It's great if your team comes up with a list of fantastic ideas, but that great opportunity is lost if nothing ever happens after that.

- **Getting equal involvement by remote attendees.** It can be difficult to have remote participants as fully engaged as those in the room. Technology can help in this area. Use video and share electronic screens when possible to allow remote participants to give input along with everyone else.

You may be wondering how to get the ball rolling. I've used "creativity inspiring" activities and games in the past and worked with project teammates in brainstorming sessions.

A personal example from a conference I attended shows the value of brainstorming.

At this conference for entrepreneurs, we were seated in groups of six per table. We were instructed to each present a problem to the others and brainstorm possible solutions. As a project management coach working in the corporate world, I'd been coaching new project managers. I was curious how I could provide project management expertise to entrepreneurs not working in the corporate environment. I was amazed at the great suggestions presented by the group at the table. These were the people I'd wanted to work with, and they offered up great suggestions for how to serve this population. They had fresh ideas from unique perspectives outside of what I'd considered before.

Brainstorming with others, you don't normally work with can be refreshing and present ideas you may never have considered.

For productive brainstorming sessions, ensure group dynamics and atmosphere allow for freely sharing ideas without fear of judgment.

Information Sharing Meetings

Objective

The objective of the information sharing meeting is to pass information to the attendees. This meeting can be for stakeholder status updates, presentations, or education. The goal of sharing this information could be to educate, persuade, or simply inform the attendees.

Approach

The information-sharing meeting can take many forms. It could be a 30-minute weekly staff meeting that a boss holds with her direct reports. It could be an hour-long monthly status meeting in which you share project status with primary stakeholders. Or it could be an ad hoc presentation to a group of potential clients who want to know more about your product.

I once collaborated with a team that worked on a contractual basis. As the contract was up for bid at the end of a term, the CIO held occasional informal information-sharing meetings to give updates and answer questions to keep morale high among the team.

An example describing this David A. Gordon (davegordon@practicingitpm.com) holds a weekly project meeting that serves as an information sharing meeting across his team. He uses a regular cadence and format, so everyone knows what to expect and what information to provide. He describes it as such:

One of my geographically distributed project teams (three countries) uses a mixed metaphor for weekly conference calls. We start with a daily Scrum-style 'three questions' round robin, time boxed at 15 minutes. Then, we pull up a spreadsheet log with tabs for Actions and Decisions being worked by the team, as well as Issues and Risks we are tracking. We collectively update and add items, working through the tabs, and then discuss any 'hot topics' identified during the meeting. We close with a quick reflection on process, for the meeting and the project overall. Every team member participates, and the log is stored on our team site, where everyone can make their own updates. We've made some adjustments, but the sense of the group is that we're becoming much more efficient at following up and getting things done.

There are various ways you could approach this type of meeting. You might share information only verbally, telling the status and answering questions, but the information could be enhanced with visuals for impact and greater understanding. Presentations containing visuals can help get the information across. Don't simply read from a list of bullet points on a slide. This is dry and boring, and you'll lose your audience.

Make the information memorable with stories or video to increase impact.

If you're conducting a stakeholder status meeting, sharing metrics and hard numbers can be helpful. If you're working to persuade a group, then storytelling can be powerful. Tailor your approach to the intent and audience.

In addition to informing different project members or groups, your goal may be to ensure alignment among participants. Include those who need to be informed or have information to share. If the audience is too large, you may want to have representatives from different areas, instead of inviting everyone from a group.

Challenges

- **Keeping the group engaged**. If you simply talk on and on, the attendees may become distracted or bored. Ask questions. Ask for input and examples from the group. You can give them tasks, such as listing the top questions they have from the presentation. During and throughout your presentation, ask if they have any questions about what you've just presented.

- **Talking at the right level for the audience**. Understand who your audience is and what level of information is best for them. If you are presenting information to high-level executives, keep the presentation at a higher level and more targeted. If you are presenting to a project team of independent contributors, you can focus more on details.

- **Personalizing to the audience**. Understand who you're presenting to and make the information relevant to them. If you're sharing information on a new technology your company is introducing, find out what your audience is most interested in about that technology, how they might use it, and tailor examples or benefits specifically to their needs and interests.

Status Update Meetings

Objective

The status update meeting usually focuses on a specific project or initiative. Sometimes the project sponsor or customer requests this type of meeting. It can be used to align the team on progress, challenges and what the next steps will be.

The meeting audience could be executive stakeholders, or it could be different groups that might need to align on status.

Approach

It can be helpful to use data. Using progress benchmarks such as milestones gives everyone a common point against which to reference.

If the status report is across teams, ensure you have adequate representation from the right people. This is helpful if you need to coordinate activities across teams or make sure that all are aware of any coordination points or dependencies.

For example, if you're all working toward a common target date, knowing impacts or dependent activities can be critical to success. If the team is working toward rolling out new software, communicating with end users, support teams, and any other affected areas is necessary for a successful implementation. If the team is expecting to roll out software updates on a specific date, then everyone affected needs to know, and you must provide information about potential problems or considerations.

Make sure that everyone knows their responsibility for the meeting and what they are expected to contribute. Attendees need to come prepared to discuss progress, changes to the plan, unexpected changes, or details behind high-level data.

The group may need deeper communication that will need more time and doesn't involve all attendees. If so, schedule a discussion afterward with fewer participants.

Document outcomes and hold participants accountable for commitments.

Challenges

- **Not having answers.** Anticipate questions that stakeholders or participants might ask or want to know more about. Draw on your knowledge and experience with these attendees to anticipate questions and be prepared to answer. Make sure that everyone who needs to provide information is aware of that ahead of time.

- **Unpleasant surprises.** If you'll be sharing information that might be negative, don't let this be the first time someone hears it. Prepare attendees ahead of time so that there are no strong reactions in front of the group.

- **Discussing issues and potential problems.** If you know that you or group members will discuss project issues, inform those involved ahead of time. Don't let those involved in the issue be blindsided—especially if it will have a significant negative impact on the project.

For example, your team was supposed to have completed a database upload by a certain date. The project is behind schedule because Mary was unable to complete her necessary tasks due to an urgent request from her boss. You know that this milestone will be discussed in the upcoming status meeting. Let Mary and others involved know that you'll discuss this topic and how the team will adjust. This gives Mary an opportunity to be prepared to present the information and to talk calmly about the situation, impacts, and solutions.

- **The meeting consists of only reading an update from a slide presentation, with no discussion.** If the information doesn't require any discussion or the need to allow for questions, sharing the information via email might be sufficient.

- **Poor use of time**. Prioritize the most important or sensitive items first. This way, if you run out of time, you've covered the most critical items.

- **Waste time**. Don't invite people who simply want to observe. If these people aren't important to the discussion, then it is a waste of their time (and company money) to have them sit in the meeting.

Other Types of Meetings

There are several other common meetings that are worth mentioning here.

Daily Stand Up

The daily stand up meeting is a brief, focused meeting in which each attendee addresses three points: what they did yesterday, what they will do today, and what impediments they have.

Motivational

The goal is to increase buy-in, support, or commitment from a team or group. If you want to inspire others to act in a desired way, then the motivational meeting can help. Appealing to their emotion can be effective. If you know why the group is emotionally resistant, you're better able to address it. You can acknowledge the current emotion and provide information and logic on the how your changes will improve their situation. When others feel like they've been heard, they are more likely to be open to change. There may be key players who need to be involved in the meeting. Resistors with strong influence on decision-makers or customers may be key participants.

Team Building

When you have a newly formed group, team building meetings can be particularly helpful. They are valuable when you have a group that works together regularly or for a long period. The goal is to improve collaboration, trust, and rapport among team members. Bosses and supervisors should participate in these team-building meetings if the goal is to build trust and a sense of appreciation for the team members.

Teams that work well together can be more productive and successful and have high job satisfaction. It's valuable to productivity to keep teams working together toward shared goals. If you have remote team members who need to collaborate, yet rarely see one another face-to-face, team building meetings can help.

Team building meetings can be simple or elaborate. They can consist of going out to lunch together, holding a team potluck, or holding a quarterly team planning session at an offsite location.

COMMON PROBLEMS YOU MAY ENCOUNTER

There are common problems that you'll likely face. If you've attended meetings, you've probably experienced one or more of the following behaviors. You may even be guilty of them yourself.

I've listed some of the most common offenses and how you can deal with them respectfully and professionally.

If you find yourself leading meetings frequently and encounter these often, you could start your meetings with ground rules, covering the most common behaviors.

Acknowledging these behaviors up front and asking for cooperation in eliminating them will earn you high marks among your peers.

Along with suggestions on how to handle these situations, I've provided several suggested statements. If you're new to running meetings or feel insecure about confronting these behaviors, I encourage you to say these sentences out loud and modify them until they feel comfortable for you. It may be uncomfortable initially. By practicing beforehand, it becomes easier and more natural when you use them.

Late Arrivals

This issue goes back to starting the meeting on time. When it's time for the meeting to start, go ahead and start. If your organization starts meetings late, you could put a message on the invitation stating, "in order to cover all items and respect everyone's time, please arrive on time. The meeting will start promptly at X:XX (the designated start time)."

If you have a recurring meeting in which participants always arrive late, you can address it with the group. You might point out at the end of a session that you'd like to start on time going forward. You recognize that everyone's time is important and you know participants have other commitments afterward. Point out that the meeting has usually started late due to late arrivals, but in the future, you'd like to start on time. Ask for everyone to help with this by arriving on time. Then stick to your word going forward, out of respect for those who arrive on time.

Caveat: when you have senior-level participants, you can't be so demanding. If senior-level staff are invited and are running late, you'll have to wait.

Hijackers

There will be times when someone will highjack the discussion or dominate, not allowing others a chance to speak. If someone takes over the discussion and keeps it from being productive, you'll need to manage the situation. Otherwise, you'll find yourself at the end of the meeting having made no progress.

If someone takes over the discussion and presses their opinions on everyone, it will be hard for others to give input, and the meeting won't be as productive. You'll need to move the discussion forward. Paraphrase what the hijacker has said and ask for other opinions.

"Sam, you say the solution won't work for your team because it doesn't support the approval process you use. I'd love to hear others chime in on this."

Ask if anyone else sees that same issue or has any different opinions about it.

You might pick a couple of other quiet people who may have different opinions and ask what they think about it.

If Sam tries to answer with a different problem or issue, state that the group is still focused on the previous issue. Address one issue at a time, rather than playing "whack-a-mole" and being led all over the place by an attendee.

When you're ready to move forward, if it seems that Sam is going to continue to churn on the same item, you could say "I've noted your opinion (or that point) on this item, so let's move forward to the next item."

If you have a large group with attendees, who tend to dominate and prevent others from sharing, using a timer can help. State at the beginning of the meeting that because of the size of the group and limited time, you want to allow time for everyone, so you'll be using a timer for comments. Asking the group to please put their most important points first will help. If you use the timer equally with everyone, it works. If you're concerned that a timer won't be viewed favorably in your group or culture, state that you'd like everyone to keep their comments succinct to allow time for everyone to give input.

Note: Don't use this tactic with your superiors or executives.

Taking back control of your meeting should be handled respectfully and professionally. Your peers will appreciate it.

Some suggested phrasing to try:

"Can someone else give input?"

"That's a valid point. It would be great to get input from others as well. Can anyone else share your thoughts?"

"I want to make sure we hear from others on this point."

"What does everyone else think about that idea?"

"Because of time constraints, we should move forward with the agenda. Let's put that in the 'Parking Lot' and come back to it at a later time."

"You've presented an interesting point. What do others have to offer on this?"

"We need to keep moving forward."

"I've captured that point. Let's move forward and hear from others."

Note: if you'll be breaking your meeting attendees into working groups, be aware if you have participants who tend to dominate the conversation. If you break up into groups with a dominator in each cluster, each dominator will likely take over each group. One approach is to group the particularly verbal members together, and the quieter ones together. Have time limits for small group work and then bring everyone back together to share their ideas. It could be a short 10-minute group session work, and then all come back together to share.

Multitaskers

You may have people who continue to work on their laptops or check their phones constantly during the meeting. Lay out ground rules or define a group agreement at the beginning of the meeting. Time and attention are the most valuable things we have. "I appreciate that you're all here, and respect your time. To ensure we all respect each other's time, let's make an agreement to one another that we won't do other work or check email during this meeting."

Ask that participants to respect their peers by staying focused on the meeting, giving input and helping to move things forward. If participants are focused on other work, they are not fully focused on the meeting. Communication suffers.

If you have someone who continues to work or check their phone throughout the meeting, how you handle it will depend on the dynamics and position hierarchy. If it's your boss or position superiors, you'll likely have to let it slide. If it's a peer, you could say "Jane, what's your opinion on this?" or some other similar type of question that draws them into the discussion.

My friend Chris offered this experience she had in a meeting with her CEO:

Once I was in a meeting, and I was explaining something. The CEO started looking through some papers, so I just shut up and watched politely. So did everyone else. He got flustered for a minute but didn't do it again. He really needed to understand what I was explaining because it was pretty much his decision to make.

Conflict

I hope you never experience conflict like the conference room scene in *Elf* when Miles Finch runs across the conference table and takes Buddy the Elf down. There can be differing opinions and discussions can get heated. Watch for cues that you should redirect the conversation.

Don't stifle conflict at the first indication. It can be beneficial for team members to respectfully share differing opinions. By using your emotional intelligence, you'll be better attuned if emotions get heated. In addition to the words that are said, listen to the tone of voice and watch body language for cues that a situation might be getting heated. Pay attention to the emotional atmosphere in the room. Watch for clues telling you if the group is stressed or worried. Facial expressions indicating agitation, fidgeting and restless behavior can indicate frustration or heightening emotion.

If you have attendees who have a history of conflict, be alert and watch the dynamics throughout the meeting.

If there's unhelpful conflict that's veering off-topic, bring the group back to the agenda.

If you're discussing a topic and the disagreement starts to get heated or doesn't move forward, bridge the difference or suggest that you move forward if the group cannot.

Circular or Repetitive Discussion

If the discussion is not moving forward, point this out to the group. Say something like, "It seems we're not making progress on this topic."

Identify the reason you can't move forward. If it's because someone has hijacked the discussion, then say you've noted the participant's input and are moving forward.

If input or additional information is needed, acknowledge that you won't be able to make a decision on that point during this meeting, identify next steps, then move to the next topic.

Silence

If you fail to get any input at all from participants, wait silently for about one minute. Give them time to think. People will become uncomfortable with the silence and want to say something. If no one speaks after a minute, try prompting with different questions to get the discussion moving.

If this doesn't work, then call someone by name and rephrase the question in a way that will be easy for them to answer. It may be that someone needs to get it moving for everyone to feel more comfortable speaking up. It can easily happen in large groups as soon as you ask for input. No one wants to be the first to speak. Ask a specific person for his or her opinion, then others will put up their hands.

Going off Topic

If you have conversation that veers off topic, you can easily bring it back on point. By keeping the agenda visible, you can reference the focus of the discussion. Use the "Parking Lot" technique explained previously. If the conversation isn't related to anything that needs to be captured for follow-up, say that for the sake of time you'd like to bring everyone back to the subject at hand.

Ayanna Castro, CAP-OM, submitted the following example of a simple approach she uses to bring conversations back on point. It's direct, yet respectful, and can be used by anyone.

I facilitate a monthly team meeting with 40 attendees and I found that running the meeting with modified Robert's Rules has been successful in keeping the meeting on track and eliminating side conversations.

I was prompted to do this primarily because of the culture of my company. At our core, we're an engineering company and there are a lot of subject matter experts on the project team. I didn't want anyone to monopolize the conversation and not allow all thoughts and ideas to be shared. The challenge was finding the right level of modification to Robert's Rules because everyone on the project isn't familiar with it.

I introduced the modified rules at the project kick-off meeting. They were included in the ground rules (along with starting the meeting on time, staying on agenda, etc.) Once the team saw that I was adhering to the ground rules, even starting the meeting on time without the presence of the project sponsor, it was clear that the rules worked.

To ensure that no one monopolizes the conversation I use RONR (Robert's Rules of Order Newly Revised) point of order using the following:

Interrupt. Thank. Remind. Move on:

Interrupt the person speaking.

Thank them for their input.

Remind everyone of the time limit on the topic.

Move on to the next agenda item.

Because we have so many brilliant and eerily smart people on the project team, it's easy for them to get side-tracked. An example of this was a discussion the team was having about the history of individual locations throughout the company and how we needed to contact the superintendents of each of the locations to find out unique history facts. The conversation shifted to talking about some of the things that used to happen at these locations. As entertaining as the conversation was, I knew that the conversation had derailed long enough. I interrupted the two team members talking back and forth and asked them to continue the conversation offline and to incorporate their knowledge into the report. I would rather be viewed as the "bad guy" by one or two team members, but the defender of the agenda and protector of time for the others. Luckily, I've only had to do this once.

Side Conversations

Side conversations can start with an innocent comment that blossoms into a whole side discussion. Whether or not the side conversation is related to the agenda topic, having more than one debate simultaneously at your meeting can be disruptive and distracting. Even if the side discussion is related to the agenda item at hand, it's impossible to follow both conversations at once. The goal is to have everyone engaged in the same discussion.

To stop the side conversation, you can do something as simple as asking for only one conversation at a time: "Could we have only one discussion, please?" If this doesn't work, stop the main conversation that you're leading and look patiently at the group carrying on the side conversation or interrupt their discussion. Ask them to please join the main conversation and to have only one discussion going at once. Point out that it's impossible to follow two conversations and you want to ensure that everyone benefits from the input during the meeting.

Negativity

You may have someone in the group who repeatedly says that the ideas will never work or who disagrees with everything. No matter how many different approaches your group considers, this person continues to respond with negativity.

Counter with asking him what he thinks might work instead. Say you'd like to give the team a chance to come up with ideas without squashing them automatically.

Acknowledge the roadblocks they've pointed out and ask how the group can get around those roadblocks. Be careful, though, so the meeting doesn't go off course.

Challenge and ask if they have experience that tells them concretely that it won't work. If so, then ask for feedback or new ideas based on the experience. If not, then suggest that it's worth exploring.

If you know in advance that someone will be particularly negative or resistant to an idea, you could ask them to lead that particular discussion or agenda item. Having them play an advocate role or being in charge of getting different viewpoints can help tame their commentary and perspective.

You can use the following statements to encourage more support:

"You say that these ideas won't work based on your previous experience with that team. Can you suggest an approach that might be more successful?"

If they are negative just for the sake of being negative, they won't have positive ideas, but they could still be useful. Ask them for reasons why it didn't work last time.

"I hear your concern regarding these ideas. Let's give the group a chance to brainstorm and come up with various ideas. Maybe we'll find some that are good options."

Disruptive Behavior

You may have a participant who disrupts the meeting with certain behaviors such as repeating himself, interrupting, or having a side conversation that makes it difficult for others to move forward productively.

It's okay to identify the behavior in front of the group, but do it respectfully.

Use the following statements, adapted to the situation:

"Tom, I know you have something important to talk to Sherry about, but it's difficult for the group to focus when multiple discussions are happening at the same time."

"Tom, you seem to be enthusiastic about this topic, but please be respectful of others opinions and don't interrupt."

"Let's please have only one discussion at a time. It's difficult to hear when multiple conversations are happening at once."

Passive Aggressive Behavior

Passive aggression is a way of expressing anger in a manner that's disguised. It might be by denying or dismissing anger or giving the sense of being in agreement, even if this isn't the case.

For example, you ask if everyone likes the new interface design and everyone says yes except Jill, who instead rolls her eyes and says, "Yeah, whatever." Jill isn't directly saying that she doesn't like it, but she's conveying disagreement in an unproductive way.

Passive aggressive behavior can be difficult to address. When people aren't straightforward, it's hard to have productive discussions and come to agreement.

Those who engage in this behavior aren't open and honest about their true thoughts and feelings. They may feel anger or mistrust, but they don't share their feelings in an open and productive way. They avoid conflict, yet their behavior doesn't allow for productive open communication.

There can be different reasons or motivators for passive aggressive behavior, but the outcome is the same. And if they have strong feelings against the outcome, they may sabotage the results. They can undermine the discussion and prevent the group from coming to consensus if needed.

They may be sarcastic or silent. Snarky negative remarks can clue you in that they are not fully on board with the decision. Body language such as sulking, shaking their head no, or rolling their eyes can be an indication that they are not in agreement. Flippant remarks such as "whatever" can be a clue.

When you see this type of behavior, don't let it slide without addressing it. If you let it pass, it could cause more problems. There are ways to address it respectfully.

Recognize that this is a form of hostility. There's an underlying power struggle. When you recognize and address the behavior, be specific about what you observed. Consider and validate their feelings if you can. Then ask for them to share their concerns more clearly. This allows for respectful and productive discussion on possible disagreement.

An exchange might look like this:

You: "James, you shook your head and sighed when Aaron said the additional software feature will put a strain on the schedule."

James: "You guys have made up your mind. It doesn't matter now."

You: "James, it would be helpful for the group to have a full picture. It's clear that you have concerns or aren't happy with something. Please share your thoughts."

When James shares his thoughts, remain open and curious. This doesn't mean you must agree with him, but if you expect team members to share openly, create a supportive environment for it.

An alternative scenario is that an attendee is completely silent and doesn't give any indication of disagreement until after the meeting. If the behavior isn't evident during the meeting, address it at the first indication you have.

This story from Kiron Bondale, PMP, PMI-RMP, is an excellent example of how to productively handle passive aggressive behavior and still maintain a respectful relationship with your project team:

One cause for passive-aggressive behavior in meetings is a lack of trust. In companies which are experiencing structural turmoil or where leadership don't "walk the talk" of psychological safety, meeting participants won't feel safe at voicing their concerns openly and may work behind the scenes afterwards.

A company I worked for many years back had gone through a few cycles of downsizing resulting in a heightened level of anxiety and low trust between functional areas. To make matters worse, a critical product release was delayed and there were fears that the impact from any further delays would be more layoffs. I had recently joined the company so I didn't yet have the lay of the land when it came to the personalities of the key functional leads who needed to be aligned towards the recovery plan for the product launch. Bob (a pseudonym) was leading one of the teams of developers who were working on the product. While I was developing the plan with the leads, Bob was quiet but didn't appear to show any signs of discomfort with what was being discussed. A few times during the meeting I asked the question "Any issues with what you've seen so far regarding the activities, estimates, assumptions & risks?". Bob never said anything whenever this question was asked. Once the meeting ended, I walked out feeling confident that we had collective support from the leads.

Needless to say I was shocked when a colleague dropped by my office a bit later that same day saying that he'd overhead Bob speaking with some of the other leads indicating his grave concerns with the plan and that he couldn't support it with a clear conscience.

Somehow I overcame the impulse to angrily confront Bob and I decided to sleep on it and meet with him the next morning. Both of us were morning people so I was fortunate enough to find him at his desk when I arrived. I asked whether he'd had his morning coffee and suggested that I'd like to have one with him. Rather than raising the feedback from the previous day, I let him know that I'd felt that he'd been very quiet in the previous day's meeting and wanted to find out if he had any concerns with what had been shared. I told him that successful recovery of the project was critical and we wouldn't get a third chance and that I'd welcome any insights on what we could do differently. When he saw that I was not being judgmental or accusing him of the previous day's behavior he started to share his concerns. I was able to address most of them, but one had not been considered by the group the day before. I asked him why he hadn't raised it during the meeting and he said that he used to do that much earlier and had been reprimanded publicly.

When we reconvened with the team later that day to continue work on the plan, I started by thanking Bob for bringing his concerns to my attention and we focused our efforts on incorporating those into the plan.

I understood that it would take a while for Bob to feel comfortable enough to directly raise concerns in meetings, so on a go forward basis I started meeting with him one-on-one in advance or during scheduled breaks to ask for his insights.

Inability to Make a Decision

If the agenda item is intended to result in a decision and the group can't seem to reach an agreement or make a decision, identify why. Find out what's keeping the group from making a decision and address it. You may need to provide more information or have other participants involved. Identify the next steps and take action on them. Schedule a follow-up session if needed.

Background Noises (Remote Attendees)

If the team is hearing distracting noises on the call, such as barking dogs or the clattering of the keyboard, ask participants to mute their phones. Background conversations, rustling papers, and other surprising sounds should be eliminated for the discussion to move forward unhampered.

Say something such as the following:

"We're hearing background noises. Please mute your phones."

"Whoever is typing on your keyboard, please mute your phone."

Meeting Forwarded to Others

Once you schedule a meeting and send out the invitations, you can't control what others do. They can forward it on one or many times. It's likely driven by good intentions but can result in various problems.

If you're constrained by meeting room size and capacity or if you're providing food for a specific number of attendees, then locking down the number of attendees is important for planning.

Worse is having attendees who were forwarded the invitation, show up at the meeting, but aren't sure why they are there, or what they are supposed to contribute. It becomes a waste of time for them. It can derail your meeting if you have to catch them up on project history and answer questions you've covered in previous meetings.

If the meeting is scheduled to cover sensitive topics or needs to include only C-level executives, an invitation that's sent to many other people will generate a good deal of work for the facilitator.

A simple solution is to write on the meeting invitation "Do not forward." This doesn't always prevent the invitation from being sent on to others, but usually will.

Consider the following story submitted by Jason Orloske that illustrates the point brilliantly

As a project portfolio manager, I schedule meetings with executive steering and governance committees to review project and program requests, status of in-progress initiatives, issue resolution, team performance (or lack thereof), and sometimes even an individual person's performance. These meetings should take place with senior management in attendance given the sensitive nature of the discussions. Periodically, someone may be asked to attend to discuss an item of importance, but under normal circumstances, this is a meeting where a select group, and only those people, should attend.

When I first set up these meetings, the first line I always put in the invite is "DO NOT FORWARD THIS MEETING WITHOUT DISCUSSING WITH ME." An early mentor of mine taught me this valuable lesson. The people invited have been carefully identified and more often than not I've had a couple meetings with them about why they've been identified as a contributor.

There are those few, who no matter how much I've talked to them, will forward the meeting notice to people who shouldn't attend. They may do it because they want assistance from those closer to information, may not want to make decisions and be accountable, or they may not feel the meeting is important. Then, the people who the meeting was forwarded to will forward to others, and more forwards, until a meeting that started out with eight attendees turns into 28 and loses its intent.

What happens next can take countless hours you will never get back. It starts with the governance or steering committee member who did the initial forward, talking to them about why they did it and asking for their commitment not to do it again. Then, I talk to each person the meeting was forwarded to and tell them the meeting's intent. I then remove them from the meeting invite. Most will understand and thank you for the information. Others will argue and feel they have the right to attend. In these instances, a project/program sponsor or other executive may be needed to convince them otherwise. Though it sounds easy in theory, it takes a lot of time in practice.

You've painstakingly identified attendees, tactfully removed those who shouldn't be there, and you're finally ready. As the team gathers, either in a room or on the phone, you feel happy that a productive meeting is about to take place. Then, out of the blue, someone who shouldn't be there arrives. You'll have to answer the WHY question later, but for now need to quickly remove them. In person is easier than virtually. With a smile, I politely ask them for a word, privately, and state the meeting's purpose, that their attendance is not required and ask them to leave. If needed, I commit to providing them a summary later. If virtual, I either try to reach them via instant messenger or cell if I have their number. In the instance I can't do it privately, I will quickly tell the person they don't need to be on the phone and will talk to them after. If they refuse, I will instant message someone on the management team for their support.

Finding the right attendees for any meeting takes time and energy. Stopping the meeting forwards and removing those who shouldn't be there is an art, and an art that takes time and energy.

Those forwarding the invitation likely don't consider the amount of additional work it generates for the facilitator or the affects it can have on the meeting.

My friend Debra knows each time the meeting invitation has been forwarded, as her email software sends her a notification. Debra handles it by reaching out to the person who forwarded. She asks for the role and level of involvement of the new invitee. "Who is this person and what's her role in the project? Why have you invited her to this meeting?" She does it in a non-confrontational way, but makes sure that the reason for attendance is well-understood. Sometimes it's a new hire who will be stepping onto the project. And sometimes it turns out the person doesn't need to be there after all. Either way, there's more up-front work for the meeting planner. If you know the role up front, you can prepare this person in advance for the meeting, rather than filling them in during the meeting.

Last Minute Declines or No Response

If a person's participation is critical to the meeting success, a last-minute meeting refusal can cause additional work for the organizer and inconvenience the attendees. It may be unavoidable, but it could be that the invitee wasn't aware how critical his role is to the meeting.

Irwan Yulianto shared this experience with last minute meeting refusals that illustrates this point well:

In my last steering committee, there were certain decisions that I needed the leadership team to make. Unfortunately, the person who refused at the last minute was the key decision-maker. I tried to approach him personally (which is not easy for me due to 12-hour time difference) to ask if he can be around for half an hour for the meeting, instead of one. I gave him another option and asked if he's okay to leave the decision to other leaders without him being around. He did respond and proposed another time slot. In the end, I rescheduled the meeting and got the decisions that I needed.

He was the key to that meeting. The key issue was that he underestimated the importance of his role in the meeting. When I explained the importance of the agenda that I sent out, he didn't want to miss out.

Reaching out to attendees prior to the meeting can serve a dual purpose: It serves as a reminder to the invitees and it gives you more concrete information on who will attend.

This investment can save you from wasted time later. The advance reminder nudges them to notify you if they cannot attend. If you find you'll be missing key players, you can plan accordingly. Otherwise, if you have not received advance notice and critical participants simply don't show up, you've wasted time.

For a past project, I had reoccurring monthly executive-level meetings that had been planned well in advance. To ensure we had key decision-makers in the meetings, I'd send an email to the invitees' administrative assistants two weeks in advance of the meeting. We discovered on a couple of occasions that a critical participant could not attend and we shifted the date to accommodate schedules.

A related situation is trying to accommodate busy schedules. There are times when you may not be able to schedule meetings with a long lead time and the information needs to be shared with many people. You don't have to solve all these problems on your own. Work with your team to find creative solutions to your particular challenges.

My friend Marjorie found herself with this challenge and by working with the team they came up with a creative solution that worked for all.

Marjorie runs a regular meeting to review customer strategy objectives with key corporate employees. She had a hard time getting everyone in the room together. Even if she could get everyone's schedule to sync, on the day of the meeting, many people, especially sales reps whose schedules would change at the last minute to accommodate customers, couldn't attend. Marjorie found that she spent many hours scheduling meetings that half the sales reps couldn't attend after all.

We worked so hard to get everyone in the meeting because this was information that the sales reps needed to share with customers. We needed everyone to have the same understanding of what had occurred and reasons behind decisions.

After discussing the situation with her team, they came up with a solution that worked for all: they decided to record the meetings. Because they had remote attendees and were using software to host web-based meetings already, they had easy access to recording software.

Now, Marjorie schedules the meeting with a smaller group of key participants and she provides access information to the meeting recording to everyone who needs it. Everyone who needs this key information can get it and the message is consistent.

The change in approach has been helpful because we have one conversation recorded and everyone has access to that same record. It prevents the sales rep from having to call every single person who couldn't be there, and say the same thing over and over. It's much more efficient. It gives us more flexibility around scheduling without having to try to get everybody there, yet we can still get the critical information out and be detailed and consistent.

When More Extreme Actions Are Needed

Sometimes, no matter your best efforts, you'll encounter participants who continue to engage in disrespectful behavior. Don't take it personally or ignore it, thinking it will go away.

Don't continue your regular meetings with someone who persists in sabotaging your success. If you've taken steps to address it respectfully and professionally and nothing changes, escalate the situation.

This story from Moira Alexander, PMP and founder of Lead-Her-Ship Group, is a good example of this type of situation:

In almost every team meeting there was a particular functional team lead that seemed to intimidate all other team members, including the leads in other areas of the business. Each time an idea or question was raised, this functional lead would hijack the discussion, often stating their opinions as if it was the only logical answer.

What made matters worse was hearing the rumblings that this lead had been taking credit for the work of others, leaving people frustrated.

Because the lead was such a dominant force, it often left other team members looking sheepish and seeming reluctant to speak out or differ in opinion. It wasn't long before team members started using their time in meetings to either sit in silence, whisper amongst themselves, check their phones, roll their eyes, and simply not share their thoughts.

The more this happened, the more this person became emboldened to repeat the unacceptable behavior.

I left a tiny bit of room that it may be entirely possible the team lead was not aware that their behavior was having such a negative impact on team participation and collaboration. Even after I had two separate discussions with the lead, not only did the behavior still persist, but the lead further started exhibiting signs of resentment towards some team members who had spoken out.

It became necessary to remove this individual from the project for the morale of the team, the best interest of project success, and client satisfaction. Although this shouldn't be entered into lightly as a preferred solution, because it can cause disruption when there's a break in a team's momentum, the ongoing damage to the team and the project would have been much more devastating.

What was the outcome? A new lead was brought in. She was more receptive to sharing ideas and allowing team members to have input. The project progressed significantly smoother. Ultimately the implementation was completed without further unnecessary conflict.

REMOTE ATTENDEES

Face to face meetings are best for discussing sensitive topics or when you need to read body language more closely. It's not always possible to bring everyone to the same table. Many teams today are made up of members from many different locations.

To run meetings that are valuable for all participants, consider the experience from the perspective of all those involved—Even those who won't be in the room with you.

There are many tools now that can make meeting with remote attendees or geographically distributed teams easier. The tools available will dictate what you can use. Your company may have sophisticated audio/visual systems and smart boards that allow you to collaborate more easily. Web conferencing solutions allow you to share your screen with multiple meeting attendees so everyone can see the same thing at the same time.

For meetings with remote attendees, consider the following items.

- **Have the ability to share screens/web view**. To share a presentation or collaborate on a document, all attendees need the ability to see what is being worked on, including those not in the room. If you have visuals you're sharing with those in the room, make sure that those online have equal access.

- **Make sure you have both web-based and dial-in options if both are needed**. You might not always need to share screens or presentation slides. If you simply need to have a conversation, it's great for attendees to have to option to dial in via phone rather than logging into a web interface. For a short, daily stand-up meeting that could last only several minutes, it could take almost that long to get the web access up.

- **Have access information clearly listed and easy to use.** Put this in the meeting invitation. Don't make people work hard to attend your meeting. Make it easy for them to find the access information. List phone numbers, access codes, and web links clearly in the body of the invitation.

- **Video conferencing**. If you only have a few people or groups of people in several locations, video conferencing is a good option. There are multiple tools that provide this service and are becoming more common these days. There are multiple benefits to video conferencing: you can read body language and reactions of participants, you can connect and build rapport better among team members, and you can reduce multi-tasking and distractions because others know they are visible.

- **Accommodate different time zones**. Remember that your attendees might be in different time zones. Plan your meeting at a time that works well for everyone. If your team is in the US and you have attendees in India or China, plan your meeting early or late in the workday to accommodate everyone.

- **Meet remote attendees before the meeting**. If you'll have attendees you've never met before, it's a nice touch to reach out ahead of time to introduce yourself. Give them a call and let them know that you wanted to have an opportunity to meet them prior to the upcoming meeting. It will help you connect and build rapport, which can be helpful during the meeting.

- **Open meeting access with plenty of lead time.** Dial into the meeting and pull up the web access at least ten minutes (minimum) before the meeting. This gives you enough lead time to address problems. if you're in a conference room with others arriving, you'll already be dialed in and ready to welcome others rather than fumbling with phones.

- **Make introductions**. It's important to know who is attending. If the group meets regularly for an ongoing project, it's sufficient to simply have people identify themselves when they arrive. Make sure that those on the phone know who is in the room. If the group is new, have participants state their names and their role in the meeting or project.

- **Help remote attendees feel connected**. If you have remote team members who usually cannot attend in person, find ways to help them feel more connected to the onsite team. This could be brief pre-meeting, non-work-related conversation with the group to make everyone feel more engaged.

I had an offsite team member who was heavily engaged with the team but rarely had the opportunity to meet with us in our home office. At the beginning of phone meetings, I took a picture of the team and sent it to him immediately as the meeting started so he had a feel for the room and could "see" us there.

- **Silence distracting noises**. It's not always best to mute all attendees — especially if you want to have a free-flowing discussion. Attendees will often begin talking, forgetting that they are muted. ask them to reduce background noise as much as possible. If you have an attendee who has distracting background noises that she can't control (co-workers talking in the background), ask her to mute her phone for a moment.

If you're presenting and holding all questions to the end, it's fine to mute all participants until you're ready to take questions. Have someone else monitor the presentation software for questions and raised hands. If you are hosting a large group, turn off those beeps that alert you when someone joins or leaves the call. Otherwise, they'll continue to be a major distraction.

- **Have people state their names before speaking**. If the group doesn't know one another well and can't recognize voices, have each person quickly state their name when they speak. This helps both those on the call and those in the room know who is talking.

- **Keep attendees engaged**. You want to have attendees engaged in your meeting and know that you value their participation. Call on people by name during the meeting. When you present the problem statement during problem solving meetings, ask each person if they understand the issue clearly. Throughout the discussion, select people by name and ask their opinion. Don't only call on the same person repeatedly. It will appear you're playing favorites. Use other components of your technology to engage participants, such as asking everyone to "raise hands" if they understand.

- **Strive for equal engagement.** This is closely related to the previous point about keeping attendees engaged. If a few people dominate the discussion, bring others into the conversation. Keep a list of attendees nearby and make a mark by each person's name as she speaks so you can monitor who is not sharing. Remote attendees may find it difficult to interject their opinions. Help them by calling on everyone throughout the meeting.

- **Remember who is not in the room**. To help on-site attendees remember that there are remote attendees, have their names and locations visible on a whiteboard or on a paper list.

- **Have a shared document to work from.** If you want contributions for collaboration, use a shared document that all attendees can modify. This works the same as a whiteboard in a conference room, but is a technology all can use. For example, having a document on Google docs that everyone can edit allows for full participation.

- **Allow silence**. When you can see meeting attendees, it's easy to tell if the group is silent because they are pondering a problem and thinking about solutions and options. It's harder to know this when you can't see everyone. When you put out a question to the group and no one speaks up right away, don't feel compelled to immediately fill the silence. Instead, say something like, "I'll allow a moment for everyone to think about that." This makes it clear that you're comfortable letting the group reflect before speaking. After a moment or two, ask the group what ideas they came up with and let people speak.

- **Getting clear agreement from attendees on decisions**. If you're making a decision, be clear that remote attendees have input. Call on them by name. Ask each person by name, "John, do you agree with the proposed decision?" "Sarah, are you in agreement?"

- **If you have more than one location with groups of on-site attendees, have a point person at each location.** Let's

137

say you have a team from Memphis meeting with a group from Seattle and one from New Orleans. If each of these groups are coming together in a physical meeting room, it's helpful to have someone coordinate remote locations and audio/visual needs and "read the room." They can speak for the room if needed. If they sense the body language in the room says attendees are confused, they can speak up and ask for clarification or other needs.

- **Make sure remote attendees can follow easily**. If you've had to send out a presentation rather than everyone viewing from the same online document, make sure remote attendees know which slide or document you're all looking at or working from at the time.

- **Restate in-room questions for those on the call**. If you have a large group on-site and someone far from the phone speaker asks a question, restate it for the benefit of those on the call. Make sure they know the question you're answering or the issue being addressed in case it wasn't clearly audible to them on the phone.

- **Ask remote attendees if they have questions or comments**. If the discussion is lively and people in the room are dominating the discussion, make sure that there's space for those attending virtually to contribute. Ask directly if those on the call have questions or comments or anything to contribute at the moment. If no one speaks, this might be a good time to call on them by name.

- **If it's critical that you have a record of attendees, use a tool that provides a report of attendees**. If you will report more formally on who attended, use a tool that provides this for you. There are meeting platforms that send a post-meeting report of who registered and attended and the times they joined and left the meeting.

- **Get feedback**. Find out if there are things that the attendees found particularly helpful or if there are things that could be done better to improve the meeting experience next time.

What if you're the one who is remote?

- **Location**. Find a location with few background noises and distractions. If you're working from a coffee shop, there will be background noise. If you're working from home, make sure your environment is noise and distraction free. If your dogs bark at the mail carrier while you're leading a meeting, you'll likely stop and apologize and it will disrupt the meeting flow. Avoid these problems altogether eliminating these issues before they happen. I'm not suggesting that you eliminate the dogs. but rather that you set up the situation so that you won't have these interruptions on your call.

PROFESSIONAL PRESENCE AND COMMUNICATION SKILLS

When you think of running great meetings, you likely only think about how to get the right people in the room and lay out an agenda. There's that and more, as discussed in earlier sections. By doing the activities in the earlier chapters, you'll already be ahead of many who hold meetings.

You can take your facilitation skills to the next level if you focus on your professional presence and communication skills.

Your professional presence is the combination of your behaviors that convey credibility and competence. This is important because it affects how seriously others take you, the level of trust they place in you, and your ability to grow in your career. If you want to use meeting facilitation to develop your career, take these suggestions seriously. If you believe you're already doing well in your career, you may find some areas here where you can improve.

There are multiple elements of professional presence to consider: poise, confidence, communication, and respect. The way you dress, speak, and carry yourself will influence how others perceive you.

Many value warmth, charm, and charisma, but inner calm is important. Staying calm through unexpected challenges will help you project stronger professional presence.

Integrity plays a large role in professional presence. You build trust among your peers when you honor your commitments and align your behavior with your words. In the earlier chapters, we talked about following up on action items and next steps. By doing what you say you'll do, you build trust and demonstrate credibility.

How you speak and communicate are part of your professional presence. Good communication skills will help you not only in meeting facilitation, but in many other areas of your professional career and your life in general. Not all meetings are made up of a room full of people. You'll often have interactions with smaller groups, or one-on-one. Knowing how to navigate those interactions with stellar communication skills will serve you well. Using active listening skills and knowing when to dig deeper or draw more information out of someone can provide insight that can be helpful to your project.

Tact is important. Don't embarrass your meeting attendees with insensitive comments.

Meshell Tingle shared the following story about working for a well-respected publishing company:

Our VP of production, who I liked and respected, had the Art Directors in a meeting discussing what projects each of us had to do that week. At the time, I was eight to nine months pregnant. Never known for his tact, the VP starts off with me, 'So how dilated are you, Meshell?' I wanted to crawl under my chair from embarrassment.

Let's address several elements of communication and professional presence to consider when leading meetings.

Confidence

For those of you who are new to meeting facilitation and nervous about leading your meeting, it's worthwhile to address nerves and work to increase your confidence.

Robert shared with me that he was new to running meetings. He loved his work. However, whenever he was in meetings with more experienced peers or managers, he felt like he didn't have enough experience to lead the meeting. He felt insecure about his abilities and doubted himself.

Remember that the participants want you to succeed. You likely have a friendly audience. The goal is to have attendees focused on the agenda items rather than on your performance. They'll be more concerned with the discussion topics than with judging how you're doing.

You can channel any nervous energy to help you have a great meeting. Turn it to motivation to carry out activities needed to prepare. Turn it into the enthusiasm that you'll bring to the table to host a great discussion and focused meeting session.

Some stress is useful. It can push you to take the actions necessary to have a successful meeting. One of my college professors once pointed out that if we never experienced stress over exams, we might not study. I interpret pre-meeting stress as a positive motivator to prepare well.

If you are a new facilitator who might be particularly nervous, practice running through your agenda. Speak words aloud that you might say to introduce each new agenda topic. As you repeat the words, you'll feel more comfortable. Visit the room where you'll hold the meeting and envision yourself successfully and calmly running the meeting. Doing this will make it seem more familiar at the time you run the meeting because you'll have done it several times in your head already.

Over time there will be less need to do this, as it will become more natural for you.

If you're new in your career and doubt your value or contribution to the team, you might have a case of Imposter Syndrome. Imposter Syndrome is the belief that you don't know what you're doing, even if you're educated and trained. It's the belief that others will think you're a fraud. It's common and many highly accomplished people experience it.

To combat imposter syndrome, try some of these approaches:

- **Identify and challenge the negative thoughts**. Recognize the relationship between thoughts, feelings and behavior. If you tell yourself that you're not qualified, then you will begin to feel inadequate and act accordingly. Identify the thoughts that come up when you experience the self-doubt. Look at these objectively and challenge them with more positive self-affirming thoughts, such as the fact that you've been chosen to lead this group.

- **Recognize that you are a work in progress**. You won't know everything, but neither does anyone else. You're constantly learning, and failures are opportunities to grow.

- **Focus on what you bring to the table**. You have a unique combination of experience and perspective. No one else can be exactly like you. This gives you unique value that no one else has.

- **Accept compliments.** When someone compliments your work, accept it graciously and recognize that you have done something worth praise. When the meeting is over, if someone tells you that you did a good job, acknowledge it and say "thank you."

- **List your accomplishments**. Recognize all that you've succeeded in or managed to overcome. In addition to your past accomplishments, you can lead this group in a productive meeting.

- **Focus on helping others.** When you take the focus off yourself, and offer support and value to others on your team, you not only lessen the stress of self-doubt but you gain confidence by adding value and helping others succeed. Bring your attention on the success of the meeting and of the project overall.

These meetings will be opportunities to get better and better over time. You might ask a trusted co-worker for honest feedback to help you refine your technique. You'll improve with each meeting and it will be easier and more natural each time.

Speaking and Voice

The way you speak will affect how others perceive you and how seriously they take you as a leader. Your role is to facilitate and guide discussion, which involves some amount of talking. Consider the following as part of developing your personal style as a facilitator and group leader.

- **Don't rush**. Speaking too quickly can be interpreted as nervousness or lack of preparation. You want to give the impression that you are calm and have things under control. If you find yourself speaking too quickly, breathe more deeply, slow down your speech, and take pauses between phrases if needed.

- **Don't dominate the discussion**. As the meeting facilitator, you're there to facilitate the discussion, not give a monologue. Do more listening than talking. I worked with a project manager who interjected stories and personal anecdotes at multiple points throughout the meetings she facilitated. The participants found it frustrating, and meetings took far longer than necessary.

- **Don't interrupt.** Cutting in when others are talking is rude and disrespectful. Allow speakers to finish their thoughts before speaking.

There are a couple of situations in which it might be necessary to interrupt someone. One is if someone is completely dominating the discussion and no one else is able to participate. In this case, you'll need to cut them off to allow others to give input. See the section on how to handle hijackers in Common Problems You May Encounter in Meetings.

The other time that interrupting someone might be appropriate is if a meeting attendee is saying something so offensive that it immediately needs to be stopped. Hopefully you'll not encounter such a situation. If you do, it would be even worse to allow the speaker to continue.

- **Don't up talk.** Up talk is when you end a statement in an upward inflection, as if you're asking a question. Though discouraging it is sometimes controversial, many say that it can cause you to sound less confident. Ending a declarative statement as if you're asking a question can make you sound unsure of yourself. Speak confidently and end sentences on a downward inflection rather than with a question mark unless you are unsure and want more information.

- **Maintain calm**. If you lead meetings, you're certain to encounter unexpected challenges. It could be anything from technical difficulties with a projector to conflict among participants. As much as you prepare, there can always be situations outside of your control. You'll set a more positive tone for the meeting if you maintain your poise during these situations. You may need to engage in a healthy dose of "self-talk" in your head, reminding yourself to stay calm. Don't curse or express severe frustration. The group will see you as a more competent leader if you're able to navigate smoothly through unexpected challenges.

If the group has to endure delays due to an unavoidable problem, thank the group for their patience. As much as I prepare in advance for my meetings, I've still encountered issues. Once I arrived at a conference room I use regularly, only to find that it was being renovated and the conference phone had been removed. Another time I arrived well in advance of my meeting to set up a projector and dial in for remote attendees, only to find another group still using the conference room. They adjourned right on the hour we were scheduled to start. My attendees were patient and understanding as we all waited outside the conference room. Thankfully, they'd all attended meetings with me in the past and knew that this was an unusual situation. I thanked them nonetheless for their understanding and patience, and then moved swiftly yet calmly toward getting us started.

Body Language

Your body language tells the meeting participants a bit about how you feel. Others will gauge your level of confidence by the way you hold yourself and move. Be aware of the following body language giveaways to your level of comfort in leading the group.

- **Posture**. Project confidence through body language and posture. Don't slump or slouch in your chair but rather sit erect and hold your head high. Keeping your hands visible above the table and widening your arms away from your body gives the impression of confidence. Leaning forward toward a speaker conveys interest and focus.

- **Eye Contact and Observation**. Maintaining eye contact and looking at your meeting attendees shows that you are engaged and interested in what they are saying. If you're taking notes, you may be looking at your notebook occasionally to jot down the main points of the discussion. Don't neglect to make eye contact with speakers and observe other participants to gauge reactions.

- **Nervous behaviors.** When we're uneasy or anxious, it's common for us to engage in various forms of self-soothing habits. Most people usually aren't aware that they are doing these things. Twirling your hair, touching your face, tapping your foot, and biting your nails are several behaviors that can give the impression that you're stressed or anxious. If you find that you do any of these things, make a point to check in with yourself at various points throughout the meeting. If you're fidgeting, simply take a breath and remind yourself to be still and act calm and confident.

Communicating by making statements and asking questions is important. It is just as important to engage in active listening with the team. There will be team members you may need to draw more information out of, statements that you don't fully understand, or disengaged and frustrated participants. Use the following active listening skills for maximum engagement.

Active Listening

Communication isn't only about sharing your thoughts, but hearing what the speaker is saying through non-verbal communication. Active listening lets the speaker know you're focused and interested in what is being said. Being engaged in the discussion will produce better outcomes by both encouraging more involvement and ensuring that you understand what's being communicated.

Here are several ways to improve communication through Active Listening:

- **Make eye contact** and give your full attention. Don't multitask. Looking at your phone or email while someone is speaking sends the message that you don't really care what they have to say. You're telling them that other things are more important to you.

- **Let the speaker know that you're listening.** Nodding and facial expressions can indicate that you're listening. You might say "yes" or "uh-huh" as they talk to indicate you're engaged.

- If you're not clear on what the speaker is saying, **ask for clarification.** You can say something as simple as, "Can you clarify?" or "Can you tell me a bit more about that?" or "I'm not clear on what you mean. Can you help me understand better?" will let the speaker know that you sincerely want to have a better understanding of what they are trying to communicate.

- **Paraphrase back to the speaker**. Saying phrases like "I'm hearing that…" and then restating briefly in your own words lets the speaker know that you're listening. For example, the group proposes a solution that will cause additional time added to the project schedule. One of the participants, Sarah, shares that a customer has been asking them repeatedly when the product will be ready. You might paraphrase by saying "Sarah, it sounds like you're concerned that delaying the schedule could cause a problem with this customer. Is that correct?" This lets Sarah know you've heard her concern. If you've misunderstood, Sarah can clarify. This can be particularly helpful if you aren't sure you understand or if you disagree and want to present an opposing argument.

- If appropriate, **identify the feelings being conveyed.** Statements such as "It sounds like you're worried we might be moving too quickly?" or "It seems you're eager to get this moving as quickly as possible?" can both indicate you're listening and wanting confirmation.

Watch body language. Sometimes you can gain insight through a speaker's body language. If the facial expressions or body language are incongruent with the message, take this into account. If a team member tells you they are fine with a plan but furrows their brow or puts their hand over their face in a manner indicating stress, this sends another message. You could point this out and ask for more insight into their thoughts. "You say that you're okay with the choice, but your expression makes me wonder if there's something else you're thinking?"

You may notice body language that clues you into someone's reaction even if they are not speaking. If everyone is engaging in conversation and you notice that Susan has a look of confusion, take a moment to ask Susan if she has questions or concerns.

I've been in meetings where an attendee started a side conversation with others, which clued me into possible disagreement. I asked if they had concerns about the item being discussed. They shared their doubt that the option being discussed would succeed. The group was then able to address this openly. Had I not asked about their concerns, it likely would have presented the need for more attention after the meeting.

Active Listening skills can be useful one-on-one. They are useful in meeting situations when you need to facilitate deeper understanding of issues facing the group. It can help encourage group members to share more if they seem hesitant or if you need more information about a topic. Active listening builds trust and encourages meeting participants to elaborate when more information is needed.

CULTURAL SENSITIVITIES

This book is about how to hold focused and productive meetings. I'm writing based on my experience in North America. Since communication with others around the world has become so mainstream, it would follow that business with those in other countries would expand.

Whether they are part of the same company or fill the role of client or supplier, take cultural considerations into account.

Here are two stories to illustrate this point:

Tate H. pointed out the following consideration in the Asian culture:

Ideally, you want the meeting to be succinct, but in the context of Asian culture where seniority in age and rank is held in high regard, sometimes the best thing to do is to let your clients talk things out and get everything off their chest in the meeting. It's their way of processing information. Inevitably, while they talk, they will make demands and requests spontaneously. When they do, I simply respond with "I'll take your suggestion into consideration and will discuss with the development team to see if this is technically feasible within our budget."

Asian culture has strong traditions. It's important to follow certain formalities that can be critical to the success of your meeting.

South America, on the other hand, has a very different culture, which I learned firsthand. I have a story of my own that illustrates this point.

While in the Peace Corps, I worked in local government in a small town in Chile. When I first started my work assignment, our new boss set up a one-on-one meeting for 3:00 p.m. on Wednesday. A few minutes before the meeting I grabbed a notebook and pen and headed to his office. The door to his office was open, so I poked my head in and said hello. He looked up from his work, confused.

"What are you doing here?" he asked.

"I'm here for our 3:00 meeting," I happily explained.

His expression changed to exasperation. "That doesn't mean 3:00! Go away and come back later."

Baffled, I walked back to the large office I shared with co-workers. When I stepped inside at 3:02, they had already guessed what happened. They thought it was hilarious and roared with laughter. "Oh Gringa! You'll have to learn how things work here in our country."

Over time I came to learn that I couldn't force my expectations on them of how things should work. To be effective, I needed to respect their culture and learn how to interact within it. Had I been pushy and demanding, I would not have been able to develop the relationships and rapport needed to get things done.

As you can see, punctuality is not expected in some Latin countries, yet arriving late in Asian culture is considered rude.

All this is to say that you should be sensitive to the culture you're working within. I recognize that the guidance in this book may need to be adjusted to work within the context of your environment. Be sensitive to that. You can't have productive meetings if people feel you're not respecting them. Consider the culture of the country you're in, and adjust as needed.

You can't have productive meetings if people feel you're not respecting them. Consider the culture of the country you're in, and adjust as needed.

MEETING ROOM LAYOUTS

The layout of the meeting room affects the meeting's effectiveness. There are multiple factors to consider, such as the goals, number of attendees, and audio-visual needs.

- Some points to consider:

- How much interaction do you desire between and among attendees?

- Is this a working session and will attendees be working in small groups?

- Do the attendees need to be able to move around the room for collaboration or conversation?

- Will attendees be seated for long periods of time?

- Will you serve food and drinks during the meeting?

The room layout should support the meeting goals and objectives. How the room is laid out will affect how the group works and interacts. You want attendees to be comfortable and focused on the work at hand. Determine the meeting type and goals and plan your seating to support your needs.

Use the following seating guidance for the best outcomes.

Boardroom Style

Layout: Long rectangular or oval table set up with chairs all around. If a large table is not available, multiple rectangular tables can be grouped together as a large rectangular table. This table is usually in the center of the room and chairs are situated on all sides.

This layout is best for meetings where all participants need to see one another and interact, such as discussion, debate, or team building. It supports face-to-face discussions among all participants since all participants are facing one another.

This layout works well for presentations to smaller groups.

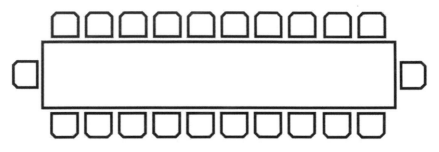

Boardroom Style Seating

U-Shape or Horseshoe

Layout: Multiple tables arranged in the shape of a large letter U. Chairs are placed on the outside of the tables.

The U-shape is good for presentations and training sessions, team building, or brainstorming.

The open space at one end supports having a presenter, yet supports group discussion since participants can make eye contact with one another. This setup is best for groups of 40 or fewer. It can be used for team building and brainstorming sessions. It's good for meetings that have a speaker and presentation focal-point, yet need to facilitate discussion among participants. The layout makes it easy for presenter to move around and engage with participants easily.

This works if you are serving food at your meeting.

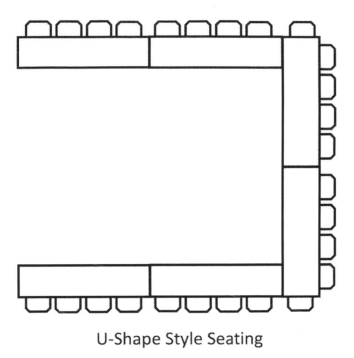

U-Shape Style Seating

Theater

Layout: Rows of chairs only (no tables) positioned facing the front of the room.

This layout is good for shorter presentations to large audiences (more than 40) in which attendees focus on the presenter without discussion or note taking. This layout can be good to maximize seating capacity and minimal audience participation.

It is not ideal if food will be served or if attendees need to interact with one another. Most people will be passive observers in this type of seating. This can be uncomfortable if attendees are to be seated for long periods of time.

If you have multiple rows, offset the rows so that audience members can look between those seated in front of them to better see the presenter.

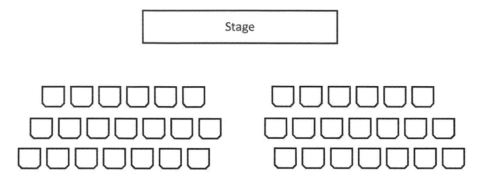

Theater Style Seating - Straight

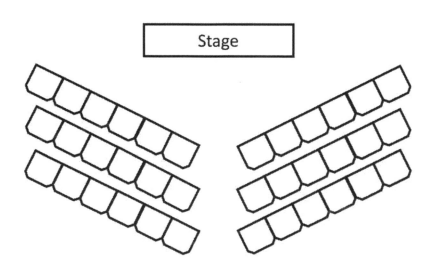

Theater Style Seating - Herringbone / Chevron

Classroom

Layout: Rows of tables that are lined up with chairs on only one side, facing the front of the room.

This layout is best for meetings with presentations for small to medium sized groups where the group focus is on the presenter. Interaction among participants is not a priority. This setup is supports group note taking and laptop use. It supports interaction between the presenter and the attendees. The classroom layout is perfect for presentations and training situations.

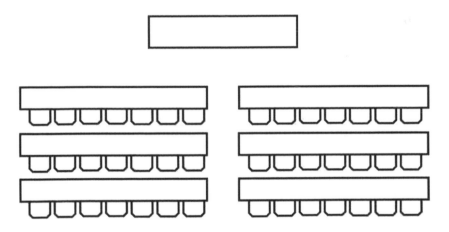

Classroom Style Seating

Herringbone or Chevron

Layout: Rows of tables with chairs on one side facing the presenter, yet seating is angled in a V shape, with an aisle in the center.

This layout is good for presentations and supports more group discussion than the standard classroom style, since the participants have a better view of one another.

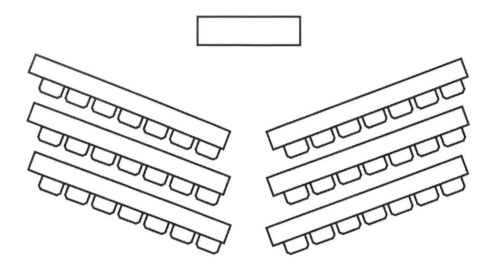

Classroom Style Seating – Herringbone Layout

Clusters or Team Tables

Layout: Tables are arranged in groups with seating on three sides. By connecting several tables together you create a larger table working space. The open side of the table should face the presenter or facilitator. This can be good for longer working sessions, as room layout is comfortable with space to move around.

This layout is best for working sessions, collaboration and group work, brainstorming, and workshops. It's good for teaching and training presentations. Clusters support interaction with a facilitator, creativity, and team building.

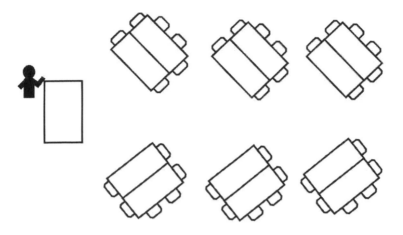

Cluster Style Seating - Rectangles

Cluster Style Seating

Banquet or Rounds

Layout: Standard round tables arranged throughout the room, with chairs placed around the table.

163

This layout is used for large groups attending conferences with a presenter and often a meal or food. It supports group work, as attendees can interact easily with others at their table. Everyone at the table can participate in a single discussion with clear lines of site all around the table. The layout provides people a clear view of the main presenter. Tables usually seat six to twelve people. Rounds easily support interaction among participants seated at the same table. It's suitable if food is being served at an event. This layout is excellent for viewing of audio-visual presentations.

- Standard round tables seat the following comfortably:

- 72" round - 10-12 adults

- 60" round – 8 - 10 adults

- 48" round – 6 - 8 adults

- 36" round – 3 - 5 adults

When choosing table size, keep your goal in mind, especially if you want to foster connection among participants. For events with meals and presenters, it's harder for people at large tables to connect and interact with those across the table from them. The large table space creates distance among those at the table and can make it difficult to hear those across the table. More intimate seating encourages connection and engagement among those seated together. If you want groups to connect, opt for smaller table sizes and groups.

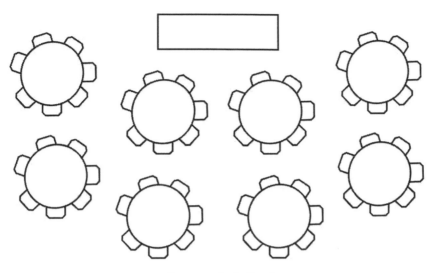

Banquet Style Seating

Points to Consider

Keep the following points in mind when planning your room layout:

- If you're presenting to a group, consider the room layout and what type of setup you'll have and the level of engagement desired with the attendees. If you want to have more interaction with people, don't have a setup that restricts you to a microphone behind a lectern. This will prevent you from being able to move around the room while speaking.

- When you want to facilitate or support discussion among the group, make sure participants can see one another's eyes. Eye contact will make discussion easier among attendees.

- If serving food, make sure attendees have sufficient table space for plates and cups.

- Adding tables reduces seating capacity. If you must get more people into the room, don't use banquet or large round tables with space in between.

- Avoid straight row seating. It reduces the ability of attendees to see the presenter. Opt for semi-circle or herringbone instead.

- Remember that attendees need to be able to easily access their seats. Very long rows make it difficult for participants to push or squeeze past others when moving to and from their seats. Use breaks or rows between tables or chairs for easier movement.

- Make sure you allow room for attendees to move about, especially if they'll need to access whiteboards or flip charts during the meeting.

Special considerations when hosting your meeting off-site at a location you're not familiar with:

- Consult with the facility manager to discuss seating and any restrictions or recommendations. They'll be more familiar with layout options that have worked well in the past. They may also have constraints or requirements you need to be aware of.

- Have contact names and phone numbers handy for emergency situations. If audio visual equipment doesn't work or the room temperature is unbearable, you'll then be able to reach someone easily for help.

- If you'll be using a projector of some sort, make sure there are no large uncovered windows that will reduce visibility of your presentation.

- Set up audio visual equipment with enough lead time to allow for potential connection problems.

CONCLUSION

There are many areas covered in this book, clear evidence that holding a productive meeting isn't a simple task. Hopefully, the points and suggestions made here help you improve the quality of your meetings.

Don't feel you must tackle everything at once or be perfect. Making small changes each time you hold a meeting allows you to make incremental improvements while not feeling overwhelmed.

Don't be hard on yourself if things don't go perfectly. Often there are situations you can't control. Maintain your composure and move forward.

Each meeting is an opportunity to get better. With time and attention to the details, your meetings will be more productive, efficient, and enjoyable. Others will notice your leadership skills and you'll surely find you have more leadership opportunities. Be the model for others in your organization. They'll start to adopt these practices, as well. Everyone benefits when you run meetings that are focused, results-driven, and effective.

Time is precious. And your project is important. And your next meeting is an opportunity for you to shine.

APPENDIX: CHECKLISTS, TEMPLATES AND SAMPLES

Use these checklists to remember details to make your next meeting a success.

CHECKLIST:

Planning Your Meeting

- Identify your purpose.

- Why am I having this meeting?

- What results do we want to accomplish?

- Answer this question: "By the end of the meeting, the group will have......"

- Determine the amount of time needed to accomplish the meeting goal.

- Create an Agenda.

- Put meeting purpose at the top, above agenda items to be covered

- List topics as brief bullet points for each item (listed as outcomes)

- High priority items first

- Time box each item

- Put the name of the presenter (if someone other than you will present)

- Make sure each presenter knows they are on the agenda and how much time is allotted for them.

- Invite the right participants.

- Who do you need for the meeting to be successful?

- Do you need those with decision-making authority? Those who do the work?

- Find the right meeting space.

- How many on-site attendees will you have?

- What seating arrangement do you need?

- Do you need whiteboards? Markers? Eraser?

- Do you need extra space for moving around or breaking into groups for activities?

- Will breakfast or lunch be served? Coffee and water?

- Do you need access to electrical outlets, audiovisual equipment, conference phones, etc.? If needed, does the room have these?

- Is there enough seating? Does the seating layout support your meeting style/goals?

CHECKLIST:

Preparing For Your Meeting

- Prepare your meeting invitation well in advance and include location and access information.

- Send the agenda at least two days before the meeting.

- Prepare and send background/supporting materials.

- Find out who has accepted your meeting invite.

- Prepare presentations well in advance. Send as a pre-read if necessary.

- Prewire your meeting.

- Double check web meeting access.

- Practice, if needed.

CHECKLIST:

The Day of Your Meeting—Ahead of Time

- Make printouts early (unless you've printed them before today)

- Arrive early to set up the room.

CHECKLIST:

Running Your Meeting

- Start on time (unless you need to wait on senior members)

- Take roll and document who is in attendance.

- Make introductions.

- Be clear about the meeting intent.

- Follow the agenda.

- Facilitate discussion, and keep it moving forward.

- Allow respectful conflict.

- Create a "Parking Lot" to keep the meeting focused and on-topic.

- Take notes.

- Capture decisions.

- Capture action items, along with who is responsible and due dates.

- Identify next steps if necessary.

- End on time.

- End early if you're done.

- At the end of the meeting, review decisions, action items, and next steps.

CHECKLIST:

After Your Meeting

- Type meeting notes as soon as possible after the meeting.

- Distribute meeting notes to all invitees.

- Follow up on action items and commitments.

- Follow up on "Parking Lot" items.

TEMPLATE:

Meeting Agenda

Meeting Agenda - <Project Name>

Date/Time:

Location:

- Invitees:

Meeting Purpose:

AGENDA

- Item 1 (presenter, time allotted)

- Item 2 (presenter, time allotted)

- Item 3 (presenter, time allotted)

TEMPLATE:

Meeting Notes

Meeting Notes - <Project Name>

Date/Time:
Location:

- Invited:

- Attended:

Meeting notes compiled and distributed by:
Meeting Purpose:

Item 1

- Discussion Point

- Discussion Point

- Discussion Point

Decision/Next Steps:

Item 2

- Discussion Point

- Discussion Point

- Discussion Point
- Discussion Point

Decision/Next Steps:

Item 3

- Discussion Point
- Discussion Point
- Discussion Point
- Discussion Point

Decision/Next Steps:

Parking Lot:

- Name – Item
- Name – Item
- Name – Item

SAMPLE:

Meeting Agenda

Meeting Agenda – Project ROAD

<u>Date/Time:</u> Wednesday, 06/10/15, 1:00 pm – 2:00 pm CST

<u>Location:</u> Building 10, Room 180/Web Conference Meeting ID 56789

- <u>Invited</u>: Jane Smith, Tim Arnold, Hector Gonzalez, Sam Burlington, Alexa Miles, Mason Jennings, Marty Young, Cynthia Richmond, Stephen Billings, Joey Reynolds, Chris Simmons, Annette Walsh

<u>Meeting Purpose:</u> Solidify web service run interval and monitoring

AGENDA

- Web Services (20 mins)

- UI Changes (25 mins)

- Identify related communication and reporting needs (15 mins)

SAMPLE:

Meeting Notes

Meeting Notes – Project ROAD

<u>Date/Time:</u> Wednesday, 06/10/15, 1:00pm – 2:00 pm CST

<u>Location:</u> Building 10, Room 180 / Web Conference
Meeting ID 56789

- <u>Invited</u>: Jane Smith, Tim Arnold, Hector Gonzalez, Sam Burlington, Alexa Miles, Mason Jennings, Marty Young, Cynthia Richmond, Stephen Billings, Joey Reynolds, Chris Simmons, Annette Walsh

- <u>Attended</u>: Jane Smith, Tim Arnold, Hector Gonzalez, Sam Burlington, Alexa Miles, Mason Jennings, Marty Young, Cynthia Richmond, Stephen Billings, Joey Reynolds, Chris Simmons, Annette Walsh

<u>Meeting notes compiled and distributed by:</u> Annette Walsh

<u>Meeting Purpose:</u> Solidify web service run interval and monitoring

<u>Web Services</u>

- Team discussed the run interval needed for web services. Because end users will want to see updated account balances so quickly, web service updates need to be frequent.

- Operations team shared that updates can be done as frequently as every minute, but will require more monitoring.

- Slow web services thresholds need to be decided by business owner.

- Reports will be handled via the normal mechanisms in place currently.

Decision: Team recommends that web services be run every three minutes

UI Changes

- End users reviewed UI mockups and requested several wording changes.

- Customer manager is out of the office until Tuesday, 6/16.

- Mason will make wording modifications, and send to end users by 6/12, with deadline for sign-off noted as Friday, 6/19.

- If sign-off does not occur on 6/19, schedule could be impacted.

Upcoming Director Report

- Director is traveling week of 6/22 and has requested that status report be given via email.

- Team members will send updates to Annette by EOD, Monday, 6/22.

Decision:

- Team recommends that web services be run every three minutes

ACTION ITEMS:

- Annette – Obtain web service threshold level from business John Doe by 6/19.

- Team members - send status updates to Annette by EOD, Monday, 6/22

- Mason - make wording modifications on UI mock-up, and send to end users by 6/12, with deadline for sign-off noted as Friday, 6/19.

ABOUT THE AUTHOR

Leigh Espy is a project management expert with over 15 years of experience in many different settings: start-up, public sector, Fortune 100, and even the Peace Corps. She's led multimillion dollar international projects and corporate strategy initiatives.

Her early career as a coach, teaching at-risk families skills in communication, negotiation, and conflict resolution give her a solid background in the soft skills of project management. Leigh also coaches and mentors new project managers and those making the move to a project management career.

In addition to contributing to multiple publications on the topic, Leigh writes about project management, leadership, and performance at ProjectBliss.net.

She holds a Master's degree from the University of Mississippi as well as multiple Project Management and Agile certifications.

Leigh lives in Memphis, Tennessee with her husband, daughter, and dogs. Her adventurous spirit keeps her on the road, travelling as often as possible.

BIBLIOGRAPHY

Hartnett, T. (2011). *Consensus-Oriented Decision-Making: The CODM Model for Facilitating Groups to Widespread Agreement.* Gabriola Island, BC: New Society Publishers.

Ishikawa, P. K. (1989). *Introduction to Quality Control.* London: Chapman & Hall.

Rasiel, E. M., & Friga, P. (2001). *The McKinsey Mind: Understanding and Implementing the Problem-Solving Tools and Management Techniques of the World's Top Strategic Consulting Firm.* Rasiel & Friga.

Robert, G. H., Robert, S. C., III, H. M., Evans, W. J., Honemann, D. H., Balch, T. J., et al. (2011). *Robert's Rules of Order Newly Revised* (11th ed.). De Capo Press, A Member of the Perseus Books Group.

Made in the USA
Columbia, SC
08 March 2019